Easy Parties

AND WEDDING CELEBRATIONS

Easy Parties
AND WEDDING
CELEBRATIONS

TABLESCAPES · MENUS · RECIPES

Patty Roper

QUAIL RIDGE PRESS
BRANDON, MISSISSIPPI

For three of my blessings—
my mother Evelyn Slay, my sister Peggy Foggin,
and my daughter Beth Roper

ISBN-13: 978-1-934193-30-3 • ISBN-10: 1-934193-30-5

Design by Cyndi Clark
Cover Design by Bonnie Dickerson
Cover photo by Tempy Segrest
Printed by Tara TPS in South Korea

First edition, May 2009

Quail Ridge Press
P. O. Box 123 • Brandon, MS 39043
info@quailridge.com • www.quailridge.com

Library of Congress Cataloging-in-Publication Data

Roper, Patty.
    Easy parties and wedding celebrations : tablescapes, menus, recipes
/ Patty Roper. -- 1st ed.
    p. cm.
    Includes index.
    ISBN-13: 978-1-934193-30-3
    ISBN-10: 1-934193-30-5
1. Entertaining. 2. Parties. 3. Weddings. I. Title.
    TX731.R57 2009
    642'.2--dc22   2009010314

Acknowledgments

Thank you to God, for guidance and blessings throughout my life and this project; my husband Richard, for love, guidance, and encouragement; my parents, Evelyn and Glen Slay, for love and support; my daughter Beth, for love, support, encouragement, and her time; Gwen and Barney McKee for support and development of this project; Cyndi Clark for her artistic design talents and delightful disposition; Terresa Ray for invaluable and diligent proofreading; Mary Graves for encouragement, support, and sharing her love of flowers and her garden; Lena Causey for recipes and for her support and friendship; Mary Ellen Lawrence for recipe testing, research, and everything in between; Sarabeth Segars for recipe testing; friends and family members for recipes, ideas, food preparation, and the use of their beautiful homes; and photographers, Ron Blaylock, Greg Campbell, Shane Carr, Bonnie Dickerson, Tempy Segrest, and David Wiggins who brought these pages to life with their talents.

Introduction

I have always loved entertaining and sharing special occasions with family and friends. These are the times that mark our lives, create memories, and establish traditions. These are the times that we experience happiness and joy, build strong and secure relationships, and learn to give of ourselves to others, which is true hospitality. Parties and celebrations help us honor dear ones going through life's milestones with birthdays, graduations, engagements, weddings, anniversaries, and births. And, holidays are the perfect times to include old and new friends and share favorite recipes and family traditions around the table.

Easy Parties and Wedding Celebrations has easy and practical ideas for interchangeable tablescapes, decorations, menus, and recipes. From setting the mood with creative invitations and simple, yet elegant, entrance decorations, and beautiful, correctly set tables to sweet dessert endings, ideas and details are presented visually with easy-to-follow instructions. Menus are provided as guidelines for brunches, luncheons, dinners, teas, and receptions. The collection of recipes consists of tried-and-true favorites from family, friends, caterers, and chefs. The tablescapes encourage using everything from family heirlooms and exquisite flowers to simple, natural elements, yard flowers, flea market finds, and craft store discoveries.

I truly hope that *Easy Parties and Wedding Celebrations* becomes a reference of inspiration that you will turn to many times to share your hospitality with ease and enjoyment.

—*Patty Roper*

Contents

Easy Parties

Wedding Celebrations

Easy Parties

Happy Birthday Hats

Celebrate the birthday of a very special lady with a hat-themed party. Set the mood with hat-shaped invitations requesting guests to dress up in hats and gloves for the party. Guests are greeted at the front entrance by a hat decorated with ribbons and flowers and enter to discover the serving table lined with cakes shaped and decorated as hats on pedestals with hangtag labels. They are arranged among lace and spring blossoms, simulating a millinery shop window. Hat boxes of various sizes display flowers or serve cheese straws and nuts. A fruit hat is made with half of a pineapple as the crown, circling fruits as the brim, and fruit skewers as hat pins. Tulle-covered hat stands display vintage hats throughout the house as ladies visit and enjoy wearing and admiring hats while celebrating someone dear.

Great ideas

FRUIT HAT

Place half of a pineapple in the center of a round tray for the hat crown. Arrange fruit in circles around the pineapple crown to create a brim. Add a ribbon to the base of the crown. To make hat pins, glue beads to the tops of wooden skewers, thread them with fruit pieces, and stick the hat pins into the pineapple crown.

ALMOND SUGAR COOKIES

1 (17.5-ounce) package sugar cookie mix
1 teaspoon almond extract

Prepare cookies according to package directions for cutout cookies and add almond extract. Roll out on confectioners' sugar-dusted surface. Drizzle warm cookies with Icing. Yield: 36 cookies

ICING

½ cup confectioners' sugar
1 tablespoon water
1 teaspoon vanilla

Stir ingredients together until smooth.

HAT BOXES

Use painted hat boxes as flower containers. Adhesive letters add a personal touch.

IN KEEPING WITH THE MILLINERY
SHOP WINDOW THEME,
USE HAT BOX TOPS WITH DOILIES
AS SERVING TRAYS FOR COOKIES.

RASPBERRY CAKE

1 (18.25-ounce) box white cake mix
1 stick butter, cut into pieces
1 (6-ounce) package white chocolate, finely chopped
1 cup milk
3 eggs
2 teaspoons vanilla

Preheat oven to 350 degrees. Prepare recipe separately 2 times (you will have batter left over in the second recipe).

For brim, prepare one recipe. Place butter and white chocolate in a small saucepan over low heat. Heat until melted, 3–4 minutes. Place cake mix and white chocolate mixture in mixing bowl. Add milk, eggs, and vanilla. Blend with mixer on low speed for 1 minute. Scrape down the sides of the bowl. Increase mixer speed to medium and beat for 2 additional minutes. Pour batter ½ full into 2 greased and floured 10-inch round pans.

For the crown, prepare one recipe. Prepare another cake mix with the same ingredients in the same way. Pour batter ⅔ full into one side of a 6-inch sports ball pan.

Bake all cakes 20–30 minutes or until a toothpick inserted into the center comes out clean. Remove from oven and place on wire racks to cool for 10 minutes. Run knife around the edge of each cake and invert them onto a wire rack right side up. Cool completely before frosting.

RASPBERRY BUTTERCREAM FROSTING

1 (10-ounce) package frozen raspberries
1½ sticks butter, softened
5¾ cups confectioners' sugar
Milk as needed

Heat raspberries over low heat until thawed; rub through a mesh strainer with a rubber spatula to remove seeds. Discard seeds. Reserve ¾ cup of juice. Place juice and butter in a mixing bowl and beat with mixer on low speed until light and fluffy. Add sugar, a little at a time, beating after each addition. If too stiff, add milk. Place one 10-inch layer on plate and ice, then the other 10-inch layer and ice. Place the ball half for the crown in the center. Spread frosting on crown. Decorate with ribbons and a few fresh flowers. Yield: 20–24 servings

COCONUT CAKE

1 (18.25-ounce) box butter recipe golden cake mix
3 eggs
½ cup shortening
1 cup buttermilk
1 fresh coconut
4 tablespoons fresh coconut milk
1 tablespoon sugar

Preheat oven to 350 degrees. Mix cake mix with eggs, shortening, and buttermilk according to directions on package. Spray pans with nonstick cooking spray. For the brim, use one 12-inch round pan and fill about ½ full. For the crown use one side of a 6-inch sports ball pan and fill ⅔ full. Bake for 10–15 minutes or until toothpick comes out clean when inserted into center of each layer. Remove from oven and cool about 10 minutes before turning out of pan. Cool completely before icing.

For coconut milk, punch a hole in the eye of the coconut with an ice pick, drain the milk and reserve. Heat whole coconut in glass baking dish in a 300-degree oven for 20–30 minutes or until the hard outer shell cracks.

Remove from oven and crack into pieces. Remove the coconut meat from the outer shell with a paring knife and discard shell. Peel the brown skin off the coconut with a vegetable peeler or a paring knife. Finely grate coconut to sprinkle on iced cake. Heat coconut milk and sugar over low heat for about 10 minutes, until thickened. Drizzle 2 tablespoons of sweetened coconut milk over each layer of room temperature cake.

SEVEN MINUTE FROSTING

1½ cups sugar
2 egg whites
5 tablespoons water
1½ tablespoons white corn syrup
⅛ teaspoon cream of tartar
60 miniature marshmallows
1 teaspoon vanilla
Finely grated coconut from 1 fresh coconut

Beat egg whites and add sugar gradually. Add water, syrup, and cream of tartar. Beat until frothy and stiff peaks are formed. Place in a double boiler over gently boiling water and beat with an hand mixer for 4 minutes. Add marshmallows and beat 3 minutes. Remove from heat, add vanilla, and beat until of spreading consistency. Frost 12-inch round brim. Place sports ball half in the center for the crown and frost. Cover cake with coconut and decorate with a ribbon around crown and fresh flowers. Yield: 16–20 servings

SPICY TOASTED PECANS

2 cups pecan halves
2 tablespoons margarine, melted
½ teaspoon cumin
½ teaspoon cayenne pepper
½ teaspoon thyme
½ teaspoon nutmeg
½ teaspoon salt
½ teaspoon pepper

Preheat oven to 350 degrees. Toss all ingredients together. Spread on ungreased baking sheet; bake for 15 minutes, stirring every 5 minutes. Yield: 2 cups

CHOCOLATE CAKE

½ cup powdered cocoa
½ cup boiling water
⅔ cup butter flavor shortening
1¾ cup sugar
1 teaspoon vanilla
2 eggs
2¼ cups all-purpose flour
1½ teaspoons baking soda
½ teaspoon salt
1⅓ cup buttermilk

Preheat oven to 350 degrees. Stir together cocoa and boiling water until smooth; set aside. Cream shortening, sugar, and vanilla with mixer until light and fluffy. Add eggs; beat well. Combine flour, baking soda, and salt. Add flour mixture alternately with buttermilk to creamed mixture, beginning and ending with flour. Blend in cocoa mixture. Spray all pans with nonstick cooking spray and pour batter ½ full into one 12-inch round pan for the wide brim of the hat and ⅔ full into two 6-inch round pans for the crown of the hat. Bake for 20–30 minutes or until a toothpick inserted into the center comes out clean. Cool 10 minutes on a wire rack, and remove from pans. Cool completely before frosting.

CHOCOLATE BUTTERCREAM FROSTING

9 ounces semisweet chocolate, melted and cooled to lukewarm
3 sticks unsalted butter, softened
2 tablespoons milk
1 teaspoon vanilla
2¼ cups sifted confectioners' sugar
1½ cups toasted and chopped pecans

To melt chocolate, place in a microwave on low at 2-minute intervals until melted, or melt in a double boiler over simmering water on low for 6–8 minutes, stirring occasionally until completely smooth and no pieces remain. Cool to room temperature, 5–10 minutes; set aside. Beat butter with mixer until creamy, about 3 minutes. Add milk and beat until smooth. Add melted chocolate and beat well for 2 minutes. Add vanilla and beat for 3 minutes. Gradually add sugar and beat on low until creamy and of desired consistency. Spread frosting over brim

of cake first and then over crown. Sprinkle pecans over cake, pressing on the sides. Add a ribbon and fresh flowers around the crown. Yield: 16–20 servings

CHEESE STRAWS

1 stick butter, softened
1 (8-ounce) jar Old English cheese spread, at room temperature
1 teaspoon Worcestershire sauce
Dash of Tabasco Sauce
1½ cups all-purpose flour
½ teaspoon salt
½ teaspoon cayenne pepper
Cold water

Preheat oven to 400 degrees. Combine butter and cheese. Add Worcestershire and Tabasco; mix until creamy. Sift flour, salt, and cayenne; add to butter mixture. Add small amount cold water until creamy. Put into cookie press with straw or heart disk; press onto greased cookie sheet. Bake for 12–15 minutes. Cut straws into 2-inch strips; cool on wax paper. Yield: 40 servings

Purses & Pearls Luncheon

This simple alfresco luncheon is held on the patio with centerpieces of moss-covered vintage purses of different shapes filled with multi-colored flowers, draped with pearls and accented with vintage items. Small moss-covered, opened compacts with names penned in red permanent marker to resemble "lipstick" on the mirrors serve as place cards. The tops of the lipstick tubes are glued to the edge of the mirror to create tiny vases for a few flowers at each setting. Beautiful round placemats, made by placing fabric between two glass circles held together with braid around the edges, add extra flair to the inviting table. The menu is as refreshing as the setting with chicken salad and a lemon dessert that is as light as air. This easy menu can be made ahead and will keep the hostess out of the kitchen and with the guests when the plates are served.

Menu

CRANBERRY CHICKEN SALAD
MARMALADE CARROTS
ASPARAGUS WITH LEMON-MUSTARD
   SAUCE
FRESH SEASONAL FRUIT
CHEESE-STUFFED BAGUETTE
WHITE GRAPE JUICE PUNCH
LEMON FREEZE
MYSTERY PIE

CRANBERRY CHICKEN SALAD

4 cups cooked, chopped chicken breasts
2 medium apples, chopped into ½-inch pieces
1½ cups dried cranberries
1 cup thinly sliced celery
1 cup chopped walnuts
1½ cups mayonnaise
3 teaspoons fresh lime juice
½ teaspoon curry powder
For garnish: leaf lettuce

Combine first 5 ingredients in a large bowl and set aside. Combine mayonnaise, lime juice, and curry powder; add to chicken mixture, stirring well. Chill thoroughly. Serve on leaf lettuce. Yield: 8 servings

MARMALADE CARROTS

4 cups carrots, peeled and sliced
⅓ cup orange juice
½ teaspoon salt
¼ teaspoon ginger
⅓ cup orange marmalade
1 tablespoon butter

Combine carrots, juice, salt, ginger, and marmalade. Place in casserole and dot with butter. Cover and heat in microwave on high for 7–9 minutes. Stir after 5 minutes. Yield: 6–8 servings

ASPARAGUS WITH LEMON-MUSTARD SAUCE

2 (1-pound) bunches asparagus, trimmed
1 cup mayonnaise
2 tablespoons fresh lemon juice
2 tablespoons prepared yellow mustard
1½ teaspoons sugar

Steam asparagus 5–8 minutes in vegetable steamer. Remove and immediately plunge into ice water. Drain and set aside.

Make sauce by combining mayonnaise, lemon juice, mustard, and sugar with a wire whisk. Taste and add more lemon juice, if needed. Pour over asparagus. Yield: 8–10 servings

CHEESE-STUFFED BAGUETTE

1 cup grated Swiss cheese
1 cup grated Parmesan cheese
1½ sticks unsalted butter, softened
½ cup finely chopped pistachio nuts
1 loaf fresh French baguette

In a food processor, mix cheeses and butter about 30 seconds until thick paste is formed. Stir in pistachio nuts. Slice bread crosswise into 3 or 4 sections. Pull out soft insides and stuff with cheese mixture. Re-form into single loaf. Wrap in plastic wrap and chill. Slice into ½-inch pieces. Yield: 8 servings

SMALL EVENING BAGS ARE PRETTY
AND USEFUL GIFTS FOR GUESTS.

White Grape Juice Punch

1 quart white grape juice, chilled
2 quarts ginger ale, chilled

Mix and serve. Yield: 9–10 servings

Lemon Freeze

CRUST

1 stick margarine, melted
1 cup finely chopped pecans
1½ cups finely crumbled vanilla wafers

Combine melted margarine, pecans, and vanilla wafer crumbs with a pastry blender until it is the texture of cornmeal. Pat into the bottom of a 9x13-inch pan. Bake at 375 degrees for 7 minutes in an oven that has not been preheated. Set aside.

FILLING

1 (8-ounce) package cream cheese, softened
1 cup confectioners' sugar
1 teaspoon lemon flavoring
1 teaspoon lemon zest
1 (12-ounce) container whipped topping
For garnish: whipped topping, grated lemon rind, and
  fresh mint

Beat cream cheese, confectioners' sugar, lemon flavoring, and lemon zest with a mixer until smooth. Fold in whipped topping and spread over the cooled crumb layer. Place in the freezer for about one hour. Spread lemon sauce on the top and return to freezer until ready to serve.

LEMON SAUCE

6 tablespoons cornstarch
1½ cups sugar
½ teaspoon salt
1¼ cups water
2 tablespoons margarine
2 teaspoons grated lemon rind
Few drops yellow food coloring
⅔ cup freshly squeezed lemon juice

Combine cornstarch, sugar, salt, and water. Heat in a saucepan until it boils. Reduce heat to low and cook until thickened. Remove from heat and add margarine and lemon rind. Add a few drops of yellow food coloring. Set aside to cool. When cooled, add lemon juice and stir until smooth. Set aside.

Cut into small squares and garnish with whipped topping, mint, and grated lemon rind. Yield: 12–16 servings

Mystery Pie

3 egg whites
¾ cup sugar
1 teaspoon vanilla
1 sleeve round butter crackers, crushed
1 cup chopped pecans
1 (8-ounce) container whipped topping
2 (.74-ounce) packages instant hot chocolate mix

Preheat oven to 350 degrees. Beat egg whites until still. Gradually add sugar and vanilla. Fold in crackers and pecans. Pour into greased pie pan and bake for 30 minutes. Cool. Stir hot chocolate mixes into whipped topping and spread into cool crust. Chill. Yield: 6–8 servings

Easter Luncheon

On Easter we remember the death and resurrection of our Savior, and spring is all around us with fresh budding branches and blooming bulbs presenting rebirth. Share time with family and friends enjoying fellowship and Sunday lunch, dying and hiding eggs, and making and filling baskets. Greet guests with a basket of colorful, spring flowers on the front door. Place small, fresh nosegays, baskets of plants, or painted chick feeders with flowers on the table and dress stuffed eggs as Easter eggs with cream cheese. After lunch, hide eggs and enjoy an afternoon with children of all ages. End the afternoon with the Amaretto Freeze and Toffee Cookies for dessert and a basketful of precious memories.

CHICKEN AND RICE CASSEROLE
BROCCOLI AND HORSERADISH SAUCE
FROZEN FRUIT SALAD
HERBED CRESCENT ROLLS
STUFFED EASTER EGGS
AMARETTO FREEZE WITH TOFFEE
  COOKIES

CHICKEN AND RICE CASSEROLE

2 cups cooked, chopped chicken
1 (10.75-ounce) can cream of chicken soup
¾ cup mayonnaise
1 cup rice, cooked in chicken broth
1 tablespoon lemon juice
½ cup butter, melted
1 stack round butter crackers, crushed

Preheat oven to 350 degrees. Combine chicken, soup, mayonnaise, rice, and lemon juice. Pour into a greased casserole dish. Combine butter and crushed crackers; sprinkle on top of casserole. Bake for 30 minutes. Yield: 8 servings

BROCCOLI AND HORSERADISH SAUCE

2 large bunches fresh broccoli
Salt to taste

Wash and trim broccoli; cook in boiling water for 8–10 minutes or until crisp-tender. Drain; season with salt.

HORSERADISH SAUCE

½ stick butter, melted
¾ cup mayonnaise
1½ tablespoons horseradish
¼ teaspoon salt
¼ teaspoon dry mustard
½ teaspoon red pepper

Combine ingredients and spoon over broccoli. Sauce will keep in refrigerator a month. Yield: 1¼ cups

FROZEN FRUIT SALAD

1 (16-ounce) carton sour cream
2 tablespoons lemon juice
¾ cup sugar
⅛ teaspoon salt
3 bananas, mashed
1 (8-ounce) can crushed pineapple, not drained
¼ cup chopped maraschino cherries with juice
¼ cup chopped pecans
For garnish: whipped topping, cherries, and mint

Combine all ingredients and pour into lined muffin tins; freeze. To serve, place on lettuce leaf and garnish with whipped topping, cherry, and mint. Yield: 12 servings

HERBED CRESCENT ROLLS

½ stick margarine, melted
1 (.7-ounce) package Italian salad dressing mix
1 (8-ounce) package crescent rolls

Preheat oven to 350 degrees. Combine margarine and salad dressing mix. Brush crescent roll triangles with mixture and roll into crescent shapes. Bake for 8–10 minutes. Yield: 8 rolls

STUFFED EASTER EGGS

12 hard-cooked eggs, peeled and halved lengthwise
1 tablespoon butter, softened
4 tablespoons chopped dill pickles
⅓ cup mayonnaise
Salt, black pepper, and paprika to taste
1 (8-ounce) package cream cheese, softened
Food coloring

Remove yolks and mash with fork; add butter, pickles, mayonnaise, and seasonings. Refill whites with yolk mixture. Beat cream cheese until fluffy. Divide into 4 parts and tint pastel shades with food coloring. Seal each egg using the leaf decorating tip to form a ruffle around seam edge. Decorate tops with lines, dots, and flowers. Yield: 12 whole eggs

AMARETTO FREEZE

⅓ cup amaretto
1 tablespoon brown sugar
1 quart vanilla bean ice cream, softened
For garnish: whipped cream, toasted nuts, and mara-
  schino cherries with stems

Combine amaretto and brown sugar; stir until sugar dissolves. Combine ice cream and amaretto mixture in blender; process until smooth. Pour into a freezer container and freeze. Spoon into dishes; garnish each with whipped cream, toasted nuts, and a cherry. Yield: 8 servings

TOFFEE COOKIES

2 sticks margarine, softened
½ cup dark brown sugar, packed
½ cup sugar
1 egg, separated
1 teaspoon vanilla
2 cups all-purpose flour
1 teaspoon cinnamon
⅔ cup chopped pecans
For garnish: confectioners' sugar

Preheat oven to 325 degrees. Cream margarine and white and brown sugars with mixer. Mix in egg yolk and vanilla. Combine flour and cinnamon and gradually add to mixture. Grease a 12x16-inch pan, and spread mixture in pan with greased hands. Brush with egg white and sprinkle with pecans. Score 2-inch diamonds with a knife. Bake for 25–30 minutes. Remove from oven and retrace diamonds. Sprinkle with confectioners' sugar, if desired. Yield: 2 dozen cookies

Great idea

Baby chick water feeders, available at hardware stores, can be painted or covered with gold leaf to make inexpensive flower containers.

Mother's Day Garden Luncheon

What could be better than sharing a light salad lunch and delicious dessert with mothers, grandmothers, and daughters on elegant lace-covered tables set with silver, fine china, and crystal in the garden surrounded by hydrangeas, ferns, and flowers? Mother's Day is certainly the time to celebrate with the beautiful things that have passed from one generation to another. Drape damask napkins over chair backs tied in soft satin bows with a few fresh stems tucked inside or carefully fan them inside silver napkin rings. Give special gifts tucked in tiny triangle boxes with notes of love and gratitude for your nearest and dearest.

Great ideas

AT THE TABLE

Tables need not be identically dressed, but do need to be similar.

Several patterns of china may be used, but each table's plates should match.

Use the same chairs for all tables. Chairs are reasonable to rent, or have several girl-friends each purchase eight matching chairs and share.

Drape napkins tied with soft satin bows and a few fresh flowers over chair backs.

MOTHER'S DAY GARDEN LUNCHEON

Menu

CHICKEN PASTA SALAD
CRUNCHY ROMAINE SALAD
FRUIT SALAD WITH ORANGE MINT
  DRESSING
CITRUS COOLER
PEACH PIE
FRENCH CHERRY PIE

CHICKEN PASTA SALAD

1 (12-ounce) package thin spaghetti, cooked al dente
  and drained
1 tablespoon seasoning salt
1 tablespoon Ac'cent
4 tablespoons vegetable oil
3 tablespoons lemon juice
1 small onion, chopped
1 bell pepper, chopped
1 (5-ounce) jar salad olives, chopped
1 (2-ounce) jar chopped pimientos
3 cups cooked, chopped chicken
1 cup mayonnaise

Combine spaghetti, salt, Ac'cent, oil, and lemon juice and refrigerate overnight. Just before serving, add onion, bell pepper, olives, pimientos, and chicken. Toss with mayonnaise. Yield: 12 servings

CRUNCHY ROMAINE SALAD

1 head romaine lettuce, torn into bite-sized pieces
1 bunch green onions, chopped
½ cup sunflower seeds
¾ cup slivered almonds
2 (3-ounce) packages ramen noodles, crushed (discard
  flavor packet)
¾ cup margarine

Combine lettuce and green onions; set aside. Sauté sunflower seeds, slivered almonds, and ramen noodles in margarine until lightly browned. To assemble salad, toss lettuce and green onions with nuts and ramen noodles, and drizzle with Dressing. Yield: 10–12 servings

DRESSING

1 cup vegetable oil
½ cup vinegar
1 cup sugar
1 tablespoon soy sauce

Combine all ingredients in a jar with a top and shake. Yield: 2½ cups

FRUIT SALAD

Seasonal fruits, such as melons, grapes, strawberries,
  kiwis, and orange sections
For garnish: fresh mint

Chop fruit and place about ½ cup on each plate. Drizzle with dressing and garnish with mint.

ORANGE MINT DRESSING

⅓ cup orange juice
⅓ cup lemon juice
½ cup sugar
⅛ teaspoon peppermint extract

Combine all ingredients, mixing well. Yield: 1 cup

TO AVOID DISCOLORING, CHILL FRUIT
IN SEPARATE CONTAINERS SPRINKLED
WITH CITRUS CARBONATED BEVERAGE
UNTIL SERVING.

CITRUS COOLER

1½ cups sugar
2 cups water
2 cups lemon juice
2 cups orange juice
2 cups pineapple juice
2 liters ginger ale
For garnish: fresh lemon slices, orange slices,
   and fresh mint

Dissolve sugar in water. Stir in lemon juice, orange juice, and pineapple juice. Freeze for 3 hours, stirring every hour to keep slushy. Remove from freezer and add ginger ale. Garnish with fruit and mint. Yield: 20–24 servings

PEACH PIE

2 bananas, sliced
1 (9-inch) graham cracker pie crust
1 (21-ounce) can peach pie filling
1 (8-ounce) package cream cheese, softened
⅓ cup sugar
1 (8-ounce) container whipped topping

Place bananas in crust. Top with pie filling. Beat cream cheese and sugar until creamy with mixer. Fold in whipped topping and spoon over peaches. Chill 6 hours to overnight. Yield: 8 servings

FRENCH CHERRY PIE

3 egg whites
½ teaspoon cream of tartar
1 cup sugar
9 saltine crackers, finely crushed
½ cup chopped pecans
1 teaspoon vanilla

Preheat oven to 350 degrees. Beat egg whites until foamy; add cream of tartar. Gradually add sugar, beating until stiff. Fold in crackers, pecans, and vanilla. Spread into greased 9-inch pie plate and bake 35 minutes. Cool.

FILLING

½ cup confectioners' sugar
4 ounces cream cheese, softened
1 teaspoon vanilla
1 cup whipped topping
1 (21-ounce) can cherry pie filling

Cream sugar and cream cheese; add vanilla and fold in whipped topping. Pour into crust, top with pie filling, and chill. Yield: 8 servings

PACKAGE SMALL GIFTS FOR MOTHER AND GRANDMOTHER IN SMALL TRIANGLE BOXES WITH RIBBONS AND FLOWERS. USE GOLD ADHESIVE LETTERS TO PERSONALIZE EACH GIFT.

Poolside Graduation Brunch

Congratulate graduates with a leisurely morning pool party. Guests may want to enjoy the sunshine and one another's company or take a quick dip in the pool before diving into a light brunch of Puffed Eggs, French Toast, Molded Cheese Grits, and Blintz Soufflé. Set the tables with bright splashes of color on napkins and cloths and simple bright Gerbera daisies in vases. Greet each guest with refreshing Orange Blush and let them serve themselves to the buffet brunch, visit and eat by the pool, and relax a bit before college studies begin. The light, refreshing Chocolate Lady Cake will end the morning with a sweet taste. Send each graduate home with useful shower accessories, such as monogrammed towels, a colorful caddy, and decorated flip flops.

Menu

Puffed Eggs
French Toast with Almond Butter
Molded Cheese Grits
Blintz Soufflé
Orange Blush
Chocolate Lady Cake

Puffed Eggs

8 frozen puff pastry patty shells
¼ cup fresh mushrooms, chopped
6 spears fresh asparagus, cut into ½-inch pieces
¼ cup plus 3 tablespoons butter, divided
3 tablespoons all-purpose flour
1½ cups milk
¾ teaspoon salt
Black pepper to taste
6 eggs
¼ cup half-and-half
¼ teaspoon ground red pepper
¾ cup shredded sharp Cheddar cheese

Bake shells according to package directions; set aside. Sauté mushrooms and asparagus in 2 tablespoons butter until tender; set aside. Melt ¼ cup butter in saucepan over low heat; add flour, and stir until smooth. Heat one minute. Gradually add milk; cook over medium heat, stirring constantly, until thick. Add salt and pepper, cover, and set aside.

Combine eggs, half-and-half, and red pepper. Beat with wire whisk. Melt remaining 1 tablespoon butter in large skillet over medium heat. Add egg mixture. Cook on medium-low heat, stirring gently until cooked but creamy. Stir in vegetables and sauce. Place shells on a baking sheet. Spoon egg mixture into shells and sprinkle with cheese. Broil 6 inches from heat for 30 seconds or until cheese melts. Yield: 8 servings

French Toast with Almond Butter

6 (1-inch) slices of bread
¼ cup milk
2 eggs, beaten
½ teaspoon almond extract
1 tablespoon margarine
Sifted confectioners' sugar

Cut round from each piece of bread with a biscuit cutter. Combine milk, eggs, and almond extract. Dip bread into mixture; coat both sides. Melt margarine in a large skillet. Arrange bread in skillet and cook over medium heat for 3 minutes on each side. Transfer to serving plate; sprinkle with sugar. Serve with Almond Butter. Yield: 6 servings

ALMOND BUTTER

1 cup butter, softened
3 tablespoons confectioners' sugar
1 teaspoon almond extract

Combine ingredients and beat at medium speed with mixer until smooth. Chill in molds until firm. Yield: 8 butter pats

Molded Cheese Grits

2 cups dry grits
1 (10-ounce) can Ro-Tel tomatoes, drained
12 ounces processed cheese, cut into small pieces
1 (1-pound) package sausage, browned and drained

Prepare grits using package directions; add tomatoes, cheese, and sausage. Pour into individual greased molds. Let set for about 10 minutes. Turn out on plate. Yield: 12 servings

USE FRESH STRAWBERRIES WITH LEAVES, KIWI, ORANGE SLICES, CILANTRO, OR PARSLEY TO ADD COLOR AND TEXTURE TO PLATES.

BLINTZ SOUFFLÉ

½ cup butter, softened
⅓ cup sugar
6 eggs
1½ cups sour cream
½ cup orange juice
1 cup all-purpose flour
2 teaspoons baking powder
For garnish: sour cream and strawberry jam

Preheat oven to 350 degrees. Butter a 9x13-inch dish and set aside. Mix butter, sugar, eggs, sour cream, orange juice, flour, and baking powder until well-blended. Pour half of batter into the baking dish. Reserve remainder. Prepare Blintz Filling.

Drop filling by spoonfuls over batter and spread evenly with spatula. Pour remaining batter over filling. Bake for 50–60 minutes. Garnish with sour cream and strawberry jam. May be made a day ahead. Cover, refrigerate, and bring to room temperature before baking. Yield: 8 servings

BLINTZ FILLING

1 (8-ounce) package cream cheese, softened
1 pint small-curd cottage cheese
2 eggs yolks
1 tablespoon sugar
1 teaspoon vanilla

Combine all ingredients with food processor.

ORANGE BLUSH

2 (6-ounce) cans orange juice concentrate, thawed
½ cup sugar
1 quart cranberry juice
1 quart club soda

Mix together orange juice, sugar, and cranberry juice. Add club soda just before serving. Serve over crushed ice. Yield: 16 servings

CHOCOLATE LADY CAKE

2 (8-ounce) packages semisweet chocolate chips
½ cup sugar, divided
¼ teaspoon salt
½ cup hot water
4 eggs, separated
1½ teaspoons vanilla
2 cups heavy cream, whipped
3 dozen ladyfingers
For garnish: shaved chocolate and toffee bits

Melt chocolate in top of double boiler. Add ¼ cup sugar, salt, and water. Cook, stirring constantly, until thickened. Add beaten egg yolks and cook 2 minutes. Stir in vanilla. Remove from heat; set aside. Beat egg whites until foamy. Gradually add remaining ¼ cup sugar and continue beating until stiff. Fold whites into chocolate mixture. Chill thoroughly, then fold in 1 cup whipped cream. Line springform pan with ladyfingers on bottom and sides. Pour half of mixture into pan. Add layer of ladyfingers, and top with remaining chocolate mixture. Chill 24 hours. Serve with 1 cup whipped cream on top and garnish with shaved chocolate and toffee bits. Yield: 12–16 servings

Honoring Father

Honor father and grandfather with an early summer supper of all their favorites. Serve Venison Poppers straight from the grill and Pizza Dip on the patio where the dads can visit and talk sports. Salmon and Wild Rice with tiny puff pastry fish are the perfect entrée served buffet style with salad, roasted asparagus, new potatoes, and grilled vegetables. The sweet ending is Pecan-Peach Ice Cream Pie with Caramel Sauce. Don't forget to express your gratitude to dad and grandfather with special cards and tickets to do things with and for them. Sharing time is the most valuable gift you can ever give to anyone who loves you.

Table Matters

SEATING THE TABLE

The guest of honor is seated on the right of the host at the table. The guest of honor may be grandfather, dad, the bride, or the oldest lady present.

Guests are seated male and female, separating spouses, with the exception of a couple that has been married less than one year, around the table.

SETTING THE TABLE

The place setting should be placed one inch from the edge of the table.

Dinner plates are placed on a charger or service plate in the center.

Silver is placed according to use from the outside going inward to the plate. Forks are placed to the left of the plate and knives, with blades facing the plates, and spoons are placed to the right of the plate.

Butter knives are placed on the butter plate that is placed on the left above the forks.

Dessert silver is placed above the plate with the tines of the dessert fork facing the right and the dessert coffee spoon above the fork facing left.

The water glasses are placed above the knives with the iced teas to the right of the waters.

Napkins are placed to the left of the forks, on the plates, or in the water glasses.

SERVING THE TABLE

The guest of honor is the first to be served and serving is done clockwise around the table ending with the host.

Plates are presented at the left of the person being served and removed from the right.

Glasses are filled and removed from the right. Rub a small amount of butter on the pitcher spout to alleviate drips when filling glasses.

Dishes are passed to the right at the table.

Only two plates should be removed from the table at a time and plates should never be stacked.

Before serving dessert, all dishes except glasses and dessert silver should be removed from the table.

Dessert silver may be placed above the plate or brought in with the dessert on the plate.

Menu

VENISON POPPERS

1–1½ pounds venison loin
1 (8-ounce) package cream cheese, softened
1 (4-ounce) can jalapeño peppers, drained
20 lean bacon strips
2 tablespoons Italian dressing

Pound venison loin to ¼- to ½-inch thickness with mallet. Cut into 1x3-inch pieces; set aside. Combine cream cheese and peppers. Spread mixture on each venison piece. Roll up and wrap in a half slice of bacon; secure with toothpick. Grill over hot coals 5–6 minutes, basting with Italian dressing and turning until brown on all sides. Yield: 40 servings

PIZZA DIP

1 (8-ounce) package cream cheese, softened
½ cup sour cream
1 teaspoon oregano
½ teaspoon garlic powder
½ teaspoon crushed red pepper
½ (14-ounce) jar Ragu pizza sauce
1 (3.5-ounce) package sliced pepperoni
½ cup chopped green bell peppers
½ cup chopped green onions
Black olives to taste, chopped
½ cup shredded mozzarella cheese

Preheat oven to 350 degrees. For first layer, mix cream cheese, sour cream, oregano, garlic powder, and red pepper. Place in medium-size casserole dish. Pour pizza sauce over first layer. Cut pepperoni slices into quarters, and layer over pizza sauce. Sprinkle with pepper, onions, and olives. Bake for 10 minutes. Top with cheese; bake for 5 minutes. Serve with chips. Yield: 8–10 servings

PEAR SALAD WITH RASPBERRY CREAM

4 firm, ripe pears
2 tablespoons lemon juice
1 head Bibb lettuce, torn
1 small head romaine lettuce, torn
½ cup shredded Parmesan cheese
6 slices bacon, cooked and crumbled
½ cup fresh raspberries

Peel pears, if desired. Quarter pears, and brush with lemon juice. Arrange lettuces on 4 plates. Arrange pear quarters over lettuce. Drizzle with Raspberry Cream; sprinkle with cheese, bacon, and raspberries. Yield: 4 servings

RASPBERRY CREAM

¾ cup sour cream
¼ cup raspberry preserves
3 tablespoons red wine vinegar
⅛ teaspoon Dijon mustard

Whisk ingredients together.

SALMON AND WILD RICE IN PUFF PASTRY WITH DILL SAUCE

½ cup wild rice, cooked
½ cup minced leek, white and pale green parts only
2 tablespoons butter
8 ounces fresh shiitake mushrooms, stemmed and chopped
Salt and pepper to taste
3 sheets frozen puff pastry, thawed
4 (5- to 6-ounce) skinless salmon fillets (4x2½ inches)
1 egg, beaten with 1 tablespoon water

Cook rice according to package directions.

Sauté leek in butter for 4 minutes over medium-low heat. Add mushrooms; cover and cook, stirring occasionally, for about 5 minutes. Uncover; increase heat to medium high. Sauté for 3 minutes or until liquid evaporates. Transfer to a bowl. Add rice, salt, and pepper. Cool completely.

Butter baking sheet. On a floured surface, roll out one pastry sheet to a 12-inch square. Cut into 4 equal squares. Divide rice mixture among centers of squares, mounding in an oval shape with ends toward corners of pastry. Place salmon over rice. Sprinkle with salt and pepper. Bring pastry corners around salmon (pastry will not fully enclose salmon). On a floured surface, roll out remaining pastry sheet to a 13-inch square. Cut into 4 equal squares. Lay 1 square on top each salmon fillet, tucking corners under bottom pastry to enclose salmon completely. Pinch edges together to seal. Brush with egg mixture to adhere. Arrange salmon packages, seam side down, on prepared baking sheet. Cut small fish shapes

from remaining puff pastry sheet. Sprinkle each fish shape with paprika, and attach to each bundle with egg mixture. Cover; chill for 30 minutes to 8 hours.

Preheat oven to 400 degrees. Brush top of pastry with egg mixture. Bake for 30 minutes or until golden and thermometer inserted into fish registers 145 degrees. Serve with Dill Sauce. Yield: 4 servings

DILL SAUCE

1 cup whipping cream
2 tablespoons buttermilk
⅔ cup bottled clam juice
½ cup dry white wine
4 tablespoons minced fresh dill
Salt and pepper to taste

Heat whipping cream to lukewarm (85 degrees). Remove from heat, and mix in buttermilk. Cover, and let stand in a warm area until slightly thickened for 24–48 hours. Refrigerate. Combine clam juice and wine in a heavy non-aluminum saucepan. Boil for about 9 minutes or reduced to ⅓ cup. Reduce heat to medium. Whisk in whipping cream mixture. Boil for 5 minutes or reduced to 1 cup. Remove from heat. Stir in dill, and season with salt and pepper. Yield: 2½ cups

ADD A LARGE FISH HOOK TO EACH BUNDLE JUST FOR FUN!

NEW POTATOES AND ONIONS

2 tablespoons garlic, minced
¼ cup olive oil
16 new potatoes, thinly sliced
2 onions, sliced
1 teaspoon Nature's Seasoning
Salt and pepper to taste
½ cup water

Sauté garlic in olive oil until lightly brown. Add potatoes and brown both sides. Add onions and seasonings. Add water; cover and steam until tender, stirring occasionally. Yield: 8 servings

ROASTED ASPARAGUS WITH LEMON ZEST AND PINE NUTS

2 tablespoons pine nuts
1½ pounds asparagus, trimmed
1 tablespoon olive oil
1 tablespoon fresh lemon zest
½ teaspoon coarse salt
Freshly ground pepper

Toast pine nuts in skillet, stirring constantly, until golden in color. Set aside. Preheat oven to 325 degrees. Arrange asparagus in a 9x13-inch dish that has been greased with olive oil. Drizzle asparagus with olive oil; sprinkle with zest and salt. Bake, uncovered, for 15–20 minutes, turning during roasting process. Season with pepper, and sprinkle with pine nuts. Serve hot or room temperature. Yield: 4–6 servings

GRILLED VEGETABLE MEDLEY

2 large onions, cut into ½-inch slices
3 zucchini, cut into ⅓-inch lengthwise slices
3 yellow squash, cut into ⅓-inch lengthwise slices
8 ounces whole mushrooms, sliced
4 red, yellow, or orange bell peppers, cleaned and cut into slices
Olive oil, salt, and pepper to taste

Sprinkle vegetables with olive oil, salt, and pepper. Grill until crisp-tender, stirring and turning. Season with salt, pepper, and olive oil when done. May include any vegetables. Yield: 8–10 servings

PECAN-PEACH ICE CREAM PIE WITH CARAMEL SAUCE

2½ cups finely crushed pecan shortbread cookies
¼ cup unsalted butter, melted
1 (12.25-ounce) jar caramel topping
2 cups toasted and coarsely chopped pecans, divided
2 quarts peach ice cream, slightly softened, divided
1 cup pecan halves, toasted

For crust, preheat oven to 325 degrees. Butter 9-inch springform pan and 2¾-inch-high sides. Mix cookie crumbs and melted butter; press firmly on bottom and one inch up sides of prepared pan. Bake for 15 minutes until crust is set and golden. Pour ¼ cup caramel sauce over crust. Sprinkle with one cup chopped pecans. Freeze for 10 minutes or until caramel sets. Spread one quart ice cream over caramel. Sprinkle remaining one cup chopped pecans over ice cream. Drizzle ½ cup caramel sauce over ice cream. Freeze for 10 minutes or until caramel sets. Spread remaining ice cream over top. Freeze for one hour or until top is firm.

Arrange pecan halves in 3 concentric circles around top of pie. Drizzle ¼ cup caramel sauce over pie. Freeze pie until frozen, 4 hours to 5 days. (Keep pie covered tightly with foil.) Cover and chill remaining caramel sauce. Warm caramel sauce over low heat, stirring often. Run knife around pan sides to loosen pie. Let pie soften slightly at room temperature for about 10 minutes. Remove pan sides. Serve pie with warm sauce. Yield: 12 servings

Fourth of July Celebration

Celebrating Independence Day is a great reason for a picnic with people of all ages and stages. It is the perfect time for an outside affair with simple, delicious food, and fun red, white, and blue decorations. Whether at the lake, the beach, the pool, or in the backyard, it is simply great to be outside with people you enjoy. Set the scene with a long, narrow picnic table under the trees with red and white paper lanterns in the branches above. The table is covered with bold, blue and white striped fabric. Blue willow dishes, red and white damask-patterned napkins, and star bowls for desserts or salads repeat the colors. Red and white zinnias and small American flags placed in French clay pots line the center of the table for quick and easy decorations that may be given to guests as favors to plant at home. The menu is simple: Barbecued Ribs, Baked Beans and Beef, Potato Salad, refreshing drinks, and, of course, watermelon and Homemade Ice Cream. Don't forget to end the day with a few fireworks just for fun!

Great ideas

STARS AND SPARKLES

Cookie Cutter Napkin Ring
Tie a star-shaped tag with a printed name to a star cookie cutter with ribbon and confetti to create a place card, napkin ring, and favor.

Fire Cracker Place Cards
Cover wrapping paper tubes with craft paper and place candy inside. Use red and blue confetti for sparks peeking from the top or sides and glue a star or banner with a name on the outside.

Menu

BARBECUED RIBS
BAKED BEANS AND BEEF
POTATO SALAD
CAPRESE SALAD
HAM STUFFED EGGS
WATERMELON SALAD
CORN DIP
FROSTED ORANGE CAKES
BERRY TARTS
HOMEMADE ICE CREAM

BARBECUED RIBS

4 pounds baby-back pork ribs (2 slabs)
Dry barbecue seasoning
1 (18-ounce) bottle barbecue sauce

Sprinkle ribs with dry seasoning and place in a sealed plastic bag; chill for 3–4 hours or overnight. Transfer ribs from plastic bag to a large oven browning bag. Add barbecue sauce and seal. Place in baking pan, and bake one hour in a 350-degree oven. Lower heat to 250 degrees and bake for 3 hours. Yield: 6–8 servings

BAKED BEANS AND BEEF

½ cup chopped onion
½ cup chopped bell pepper
1 tablespoon margarine
1 pound ground beef
1 (3-pound) can baked beans
½ cup brown sugar
1½ cups barbecue sauce
¼ cup bacon bits

Preheat oven to 350 degrees. Sauté onion and bell pepper in margarine; drain. Add ground beef; brown and drain. Combine onions, peppers, and beef with beans. Stir in brown sugar and barbecue sauce. Pour into a 9x13-inch baking dish and sprinkle with bacon bits. Bake for about 30 minutes. Yield: 20–24 servings

POTATO SALAD

8 potatoes, boiled and cubed
2 tablespoons margarine
4 tablespoons dill pickle cubes
2 teaspoons celery seed
Salt and black pepper to taste
¾ cup mayonnaise
5 hard-cooked eggs, chopped
For garnish: paprika

Combine potatoes and margarine; cool. Add pickles, celery seed, salt, pepper, and mayonnaise. Stir in eggs. Sprinkle with paprika. Yield: 8–10 servings

CAPRESE SALAD

20 sprigs fresh rosemary (each about 4–5 inches long)
1 (10-ounce) package grape tomatoes
1 pound fresh mozzarella cheese, cut into 1-inch cubes
Fresh basil leaves, washed and dried
½ teaspoon sea salt
½ teaspoon freshly ground black pepper
1 teaspoon oregano
¼ cup extra virgin olive oil

Remove leaves from 2 inches of each rosemary sprig to make a skewer. Skewer basil leaf, tomato, and mozzarella block. Sprinkle with salt, pepper, and oregano and drizzle with oil. Yield: 20 servings

Ham Stuffed Eggs

6 large hard-cooked eggs, peeled
3 tablespoons mayonnaise
½ cup finely chopped, cooked ham
1 teaspoon Dijon mustard
¼ teaspoon lemon juice
2 tablespoons chopped parsley
For garnish: cayenne pepper

Cut eggs in half lengthwise. Remove yolks; set aside whites. Mash yolks with fork and combine with remaining ingredients. Stuff egg whites with yolk mixture with spoon or piping bag. Sprinkle with cayenne pepper. Cover and chill until serving. Yield: 12 egg halves

Watermelon Salad

1 (6-ounce) package strawberry gelatin
2 cups boiling water
3 cups watermelon cubes
1 (12-ounce) can crushed pineapple, not drained
1 cup chopped pecans
1 (8-ounce) package cream cheese, softened
¼ cup sugar
1 (8-ounce) container whipped topping
For garnish: watermelon stars

Dissolve gelatin in water, and chill until slightly set. Add melon, pineapple, and pecans. Pour into a 9x13-inch dish, and chill until firm. Beat cream cheese and sugar until fluffy. Stir in whipped topping, and spread over gelatin. Cut stars from watermelon with a small star cookie cutter. Place a melon star on each serving. Yield: 12 servings

USE STAR-SHAPED COOKIE CUTTERS OF VARIOUS SIZES TO CUT WATERMELON PIECES.

Corn Dip

1 (16-ounce) can shoepeg corn
8 cherry tomatoes, quartered
1 medium cucumber, peeled, seeded, and diced
½ cup each: chopped green and red bell pepper
½ cup chopped celery
½ cup chopped Vidalia onion
½ teaspoon each: salt and black pepper

Combine corn, tomatoes, cucumber, green pepper, red peppers, celery, and onion. Season with salt and pepper. Toss with Dressing and chill for 1 hour. Serve with chips. Yield: 16–20 servings

DRESSING

¼ cup red wine vinegar
2 tablespoons extra virgin olive oil
1 teaspoon sugar
2 tablespoons mayonnaise
1 tablespoon sour cream

Combine vinegar, olive oil, and sugar and whisk until sugar is dissolved. Add mayonnaise and sour cream and stir until blended.

FROSTED ORANGE CAKES

1½ cups all-purpose flour
2 cups sugar
1 teaspoon salt
1 cup butter, softened
4 eggs, room temperature
2 teaspoons orange extract
1 teaspoon grated orange zest
For garnish: cherries with stems

Preheat oven to 350 degrees. Combine flour, sugar and salt. Add butter, eggs, extract, and zest. Beat with mixer until blended. Pour batter into greased cupcake pans. Bake 20 minutes or until light brown. Remove from oven; cool and pierce each cake with a fork. Frost and place a cherry on top of each. Yield: 1 dozen

ORANGE CREAM CHEESE FROSTING

1 (8-ounce) package cream cheese, softened
4 tablespoons butter, softened
1 (1-pound) box confectioners' sugar
2 tablespoons orange zest
2 tablespoons orange juice

Whip cream cheese and butter with mixer. Gradually beat in the confectioners' sugar until smooth. Beat in the orange zest and juice.

BERRY TARTS

1 cup fresh blackberries, raspberries, or blueberries
2 tablespoons quick cooking tapioca
1 cup sugar
1 tablespoon lemon juice
⅛ teaspoon salt
8 tart shells
1 pie crust
1 egg, beaten

Preheat oven to 350 degrees. Combine berries, tapioca, sugar, lemon juice, and salt; let stand 10 minutes. Spoon into tart shells on cookie sheet. Bake for 18–20 minutes. Cut stars from the pie crust using a cookie cutter, and brush with beaten egg. Place stars on a cookie sheet; bake 5 minutes. Place one star in the center of each tart. Serve with ice cream or whipped topping. Yield: 8 tarts

HOMEMADE ICE CREAM

6 eggs, room temperature
2½ cups sugar
2 (12-ounce) cans evaporated milk
3 tablespoons vanilla
2 quarts milk, plus enough to make gallon

Beat eggs with wire whisk until foamy; add sugar, evaporated milk, and vanilla and beat until combined. Pour into Dutch oven and add 2 quarts milk. Simmer over medium heat 10 minutes, stirring constantly, but do not boil. Cool; may be refrigerated until freezing. Pour into one-gallon ice cream freezer container and add milk to fill. Freeze according to directions in layers of crushed ice and ice cream salt. Yield: 1 gallon

FRESH BLACKBERRIES, RASPBERRIES, AND BLUEBERRIES SERVED WITH ICE CREAM ADD TO THE PATRIOTIC THEME.

Sip and See the New Baby

Having a "sip and see" tea party is a great way to honor a new mom and welcome her little one. Tea may be served at individual tables or buffet style. Serve savories, breads and pastries, and fruits and sweets with teas of choice. Enjoy the time to relax with dear friends over a cup of tea to encourage the new mom and to cuddle the baby. Many tea foods may be prepared ahead, and there is certainly something for everyone. Give mom antique tea cups to share tea with her little sweetheart over the years to establish precious moments and as remembrances of time enjoyed with friends.

Great ideas

ALL ABOUT TEA

A tea menu should consist of three sandwich choices, three savory choices with three condiment choices, and three dessert choices.

Tea items should be two-bite sized.

Serve tea delights on tiered servers decorated with ivy and flowers.

FRESH SANDWICHES

To keep prepared sandwiches fresh, store them in layers between damp paper towels in airtight containers in the refrigerator.

To retain freshness on the table, serve sandwiches in silver baskets or bread bowls between layers of leaf lettuce.

Menu

Ham and Cream Cheese Sandwiches
Pimiento Cheese Sandwiches
Cheese Wafers
Cream Scones with Raspberry Sauce, Lemon Curd, and Cream
Cream Filled Wafers
Lemon Squares
Flower Butter Cookies
Berry Spritzer and Various Teas

HAM AND CREAM CHEESE SANDWICHES

½ (16-ounce) canned ham
1 tablespoon Dijon mustard
1 tablespoon brown sugar
2 tablespoons mayonnaise
1 (8-ounce) container soft cream cheese with chives
Salt and pepper to taste
½ cup butter, softened
16 slices wheat bread
8 slices white bread
For garnish: fresh chives

Spread ham with mustard and brown sugar and wrap in foil. Bake for one hour at 275 degrees. Cool; cut into pieces. Mix ham and mayonnaise in a food processor; blend and set aside. Combine cream cheese, salt, and pepper. Butter slices of wheat bread on one side and white bread on both sides. Layer 3-tiered sandwich with one slice wheat bread, ham mixture, white bread, cream cheese mixture, and wheat bread. Remove crusts; cut each sandwich into 3 fingers. Garnish with chives. Yield: 24 sandwiches

TEA SANDWICHES SHOULD HAVE CRUSTS REMOVED. USE KITCHEN SHEARS TO REMOVE CRUSTS AND CUT SANDWICHES MORE QUICKLY AND NEATLY.

PIMIENTO CHEESE SANDWICHES

1 (2-ounce) jar pimientos with juice
1 (8-ounce) package shredded mild Cheddar cheese
4 tablespoons mayonnaise
½ teaspoon each: salt, white pepper, and black pepper
32 slices wheat bread
For garnish: fresh parsley

Stir together ingredients and spread to make 16 sandwiches. Cut into shapes with a cookie cutter and garnish with parsley. Yield: 16 sandwiches

CHEESE WAFERS

2 sticks margarine, softened
2 cups grated sharp Cheddar cheese
2½ cups all-purpose flour
¾ teaspoon salt
1 teaspoon red pepper
1 cup pecan halves

Mix margarine, cheese, flour, salt, and red pepper. Divide into 3 parts. Roll each into a cylinder 1½ inch in diameter. Wrap in wax paper and chill about 2 hours. Slice about ¼ inch thick, and place a pecan half on each slice. Bake on ungreased cookie sheet at 350 degrees for 20–22 minutes. Cool on wire rack. Yield: 5 dozen wafers

CREAM SCONES

2 cups all-purpose flour
2½ teaspoons baking powder
¼ teaspoon salt
¼ cup sugar
4 tablespoons butter
¾ cup whipping cream

Preheat oven to 400 degrees. Sift together flour, baking powder, and salt; add sugar. Cut in butter until crumbly. Add cream and blend. Dough will be sticky. Flour a flat workspace and knead dough for about 30 seconds. Roll out to ½ inch thick and cut to shape with cutter. Bake for 15 minutes. Serve with Raspberry Sauce, Lemon Curd, and Mock Devonshire Cream. Yield: 1 dozen scones

RASPBERRY SAUCE

3 cups crushed raspberries
1 cup sugar
1 cup light corn syrup

Cook all ingredients over medium heat, stirring until all sugar is dissolved. Boil for one minute. Cool and chill. Yield: 3 cups

LEMON CURD

Zest of 2 lemons
Juice of 2 lemons
2 tablespoons butter, cut into pieces
1 cup sugar
3 eggs, beaten

In the top of a double boiler, combine lemon peel, lemon juice, butter, sugar, and eggs. Place over simmering water and stir until sugar is dissolved. Continue to cook, stirring occasionally, until thickened and smooth. May be stored in sterilized jars for about 2 weeks. Yield: 1 pint

MOCK DEVONSHIRE CREAM

½ cup whipping cream
2 tablespoons confectioners' sugar
½ cup sour cream
½ teaspoon vanilla

Whip cream and mix in sugar. Fold in sour cream and vanilla. Yield: 2 cups

CREAM FILLED WAFERS

1 cup butter, softened
⅓ cup whipping cream
2 cups all-purpose flour
⅓ cup sugar for sprinkling

Mix butter, cream, and flour. Cover and chill 30 minutes. Heat oven to 350 degrees. Roll out ⅓ of the dough ⅛ inch thick on floured surface. Cut into 1½-inch circles. Coat circles with sugar. Place on lightly greased baking sheet and prick each round with a fork. Bake 7–9 minutes until set but not brown. Cool cookies on wire rack. Put cookies together in pairs with Filling in middle. Yield: 2 dozen wafers

FILLING

¼ cup butter, softened
¾ cup confectioners' sugar
1 teaspoon vanilla
Few drops red food coloring

Cream butter, sugar, and vanilla until smooth. Tint pink with a few drops of red food coloring.

LEMON SQUARES

1½ sticks margarine, melted
1½ cups all-purpose flour
1 cup chopped pecans
1 (8-ounce) package and 1 (3-ounce) package cream cheese, softened
2 (8-ounce) containers whipped topping, divided
2 (14-ounce) cans sweetened condensed milk
2 egg yolks
1 cup lemon juice

Preheat oven to 400 degrees. Blend margarine, flour, and pecans with fork and press into 9x13-inch glass baking dish; bake 20 minutes. Cool 10 minutes. Beat cream cheese with mixer until fluffy; fold in one container whipped topping. Spread over crust. Combine condensed milk, egg yolks, and lemon juice. Pour over cream layer. Chill. Cover with remaining container of whipped topping and cut into squares. Yield: 20 squares

FLOWER BUTTER COOKIES

1 cup butter, softened
1 cup sugar
1 egg
1 teaspoon vanilla
2½ cups all-purpose flour
1 teaspoon baking powder

Preheat oven to 375 degrees. Cream butter and sugar with mixer; add egg and vanilla. Combine flour and baking powder; gradually add to creamed mixture. Shape into 3 balls; cover and chill one hour.

Remove one ball at a time and roll on a floured surface to about ⅛–¼ inch thick. Cut into desired shapes. Layer shapes to resemble dimensional flowers such as daisies, pansies, and roses. Place on a parchment-lined baking sheet; bake 9 minutes. Cool on wire rack. Paint using brush and tinted egg white wash. Yield: 2 dozen cookies

EGG WHITE WASH

2 egg whites
Few drops water
Pastel food coloring

Divide egg whites among 4 small bowls. Stir a few drops of water and a few drops of food coloring into each bowl. Paint cookies with different shades and shadows to resemble flowers. Allow each layer to dry before adding centers, stamens, and veins. Return cookies to oven for one minute to set egg white.

BERRY SPRITZER

1 (2-liter) bottle 7-Up
2 regular-size Wild Berry Zinger tea bags
For garnish: fresh berries and mint

Pour ¼ cup 7-Up from bottle. Add tea bags to bottle of remaining drink. Chill overnight. Serve over crushed ice with fresh berries and mint. Yield: 8–10 servings

TEA SHOULD BE SERVED WITH WHOLE MILK AND NOT CREAM, LEMON SLICES, ORANGE SLICES, AND SUGAR.

Autumn Dinner

Autumn is certainly one of the most pleasant seasons. The temperatures are delightful, and all of the senses are touched by the beauty, texture, and fragrance of roadside berries and jewel-toned leaves. It is the perfect time to invite friends to enjoy comfort foods and share an autumn evening under the stars. Guests follow paths lit by small lanterns lining walkways and hanging from trees as they proceed to outside tables dressed in pumpkin-colored cloths. Small pumpkins topped by fall leaves and hand-lettered with names direct guests to their places. Scalloped rattan chargers are topped with gold-rimmed, green service plates draped with white napkins, giving prominence to green and white striped salad plates featuring mixed greens, feta cheese, cranberries, and candied almonds splashed with a light dressing. The meal consists of Grillades over Cheese Grits, Roasted Asparagus, and Hot Curried Fruit and is completed with Fresh Apple Cake with a caramel glaze. It is an evening that touches all the senses.

Menu

AUTUMN SALAD WITH CANDIED ALMONDS

8 cups mixed salad greens
1 cup feta cheese, crumbled
1 cup dried cranberries

Mix ingredients and chill covered.

CANDIED ALMONDS

1 cup slivered almonds
4 teaspoons sugar

Cook almonds and sugar in skillet over high heat until coated in syrup and light brown, stirring constantly. Pour onto foil-lined surface. Cool; break into pieces.

DRESSING

1 teaspoon salt
¼ teaspoon Tabasco Sauce
3 tablespoons white wine vinegar
3 tablespoons sugar
½ cup oil

Combine salt, Tabasco, vinegar, sugar, and oil in a jar; shake well. Drizzle over the salad and toss to mix well. Sprinkle with Candied Almonds. Yield: 10–12 servings

USE SMALL PUMPKINS WITH NAMES ON
LEAVES FOR PLACE CARDS.

GRILLADES

10 pounds beef round steak
1 cup bacon grease, divided
1 cup all-purpose flour
1 bunch green onions, chopped
2 cups chopped celery
3 cups chopped green bell peppers
1 (28-ounce) can diced tomatoes
2 (8-ounce) cans tomato sauce
2 teaspoons thyme
2 cups burgundy wine
½–1 cup water
1 teaspoon pepper
3 cloves garlic, minced
1 bunch parsley, chopped
Tabasco Sauce to taste
4 tablespoons Worcestershire sauce
6 bay leaves

Cut meat into strips and brown in about ½ cup bacon grease. Remove meat and wipe out pan. Add remaining grease, heat, and stir in flour. Make brown roux. Add meat, onions, celery, green pepper, tomatoes, tomato sauce, and thyme, stirring until sauce has lost its bright red color. Add wine, water, and seasonings. Reduce and simmer 2 hours. Serve over grits. Yield: 24 servings

CHEESE GRITS

2 cups uncooked grits, not instant
1½ teaspoons salt
7 cups warm water
2 sticks butter
1 (12-ounce) package Velveeta cheese, cut in small pieces
1 teaspoon garlic powder
½ cup half-and-half
4 eggs, beaten
Salt and white pepper to taste

Preheat oven to 350 degrees. Cook grits in salted boiling water, covered on low for 15 minutes. Stir in remaining ingredients. Bake in 3-quart casserole for one hour. Yield: 10–12 servings

ROASTED ASPARAGUS

1 pound fresh asparagus, tough ends removed
1 tablespoon olive oil
1 teaspoon each: kosher salt and black pepper
For garnish: stuffed green olives and black olives

Place asparagus on cookie sheet. Drizzle with olive oil. Sprinkle with salt and pepper. Bake in preheated 400-degree oven for 10–15 minutes. Garnish with olives. Yield: 8 servings

HOT CURRIED FRUIT

1 (29-ounce) can pear halves
1 (29-ounce) can peach halves
1 (20-ounce) can pineapple chunks
1 (17-ounce) can apricot halves
1 (6-ounce) jar maraschino cherries
½ cup white raisins
¾ cup sugar
1 teaspoon curry powder
¼ teaspoon salt
3 tablespoons all-purpose flour
3 tablespoons butter
½ cup cream sherry

Drain fruits; reserve juice. Measure ¾ cup combined juice; set aside. Soak raisins 5 minutes in hot water. Combine sugar, curry, salt, and flour. Add butter and juice. Heat, but do not boil; stir until thick. Add sherry. Combine with fruit; chill overnight. Bake in preheated 350-degree oven for 30 minutes. Yield: 12 servings

FRESH APPLE CAKE

2 cups sugar
1½ cups oil
4 eggs
3 cups all-purpose flour
1 teaspoon each: baking soda and salt
3 apples, peeled and finely diced
1 cup chopped walnuts
2 teaspoons vanilla

Preheat oven to 325 degrees. Combine sugar and oil and beat well. Add eggs, one at a time. Sift dry ingredients; beat into egg mixture. Stir in apples, nuts, and vanilla. Pour into buttered tube pan and bake 1 hour 15 minutes. Yield: 16–20 servings

CARAMEL GLAZE
1 cup dark brown sugar
1 stick butter
½ cup heavy cream

Combine ingredients and boil 3 minutes. Pour over hot cake. Cool cake and remove from pan.

SWEETENED WHIPPED CREAM
½ pint whipping cream
1 tablespoon superfine sugar

Beat cream with mixer until soft peaks form. Beat in sugar until stiff peaks form. Serve with cake.

Southern Fall Buffet

Fall is the perfect time with kids back in school and settling into routines to get together with friends that you've missed over the summer. A buffet of southern favorites before the theatre or a ballgame can offer the perfect menu. Serve Chicken Poppers, Oven-Fried Catfish, Black-Eyed Pea Dip, and Crunchy Coleslaw on a table decorated in warm, jewel-toned hues and sweet magnolias, pampas grass tassels, and lush green plants inside toile cachepots. Add warm cider, coffee, or spiced tea, a Pear Tart, and a White Wine Cake and the evening of fun is off to a wonderful beginning.

Menu

CHICKEN POPPERS
OVEN-FRIED CATFISH
BLACK-EYED PEA DIP
CRUNCHY COLESLAW
PEAR TART
WHITE WINE CAKE

CHICKEN POPPERS

15 jalapeño peppers
1 (8-ounce) package cream cheese, softened
Several boneless, skinless chicken breast tenders
½ pound bacon
1 bottle sweet and sour sauce

Cut peppers in half, lengthwise. Remove seeds and veins; wash and thoroughly dry. Fill each pepper with a small amount of cream cheese. Cut the chicken into strips to fit inside peppers. Place chicken piece over cream cheese. Wrap ½ slice of bacon around each stuffed pepper and hold in place with 2 toothpicks. Let toothpicks stick out large end of pepper like a fish tail to pick up the pepper. Place stuffed peppers on baking pan that has been sprayed with nonstick cooking spray. Bake at 325 degrees for 45–50 minutes or until the bacon and chicken are done. Brush with sweet and sour sauce. Yield: 30 servings

OVEN-FRIED CATFISH

1 cup crushed cornflakes
1 cup Oven Fry Seasoned Coating for fish
1 tablespoon chopped pecans
½ teaspoon salt
2 pounds catfish fillets
1 cup milk
For garnish: lemon slices and parsley

Preheat oven to 475 degrees. Combine cornflakes, Oven Fry coating, pecans, and salt; set aside. Rinse fillets in cold water, and pat dry. Dip fillets in milk; coat with cornflake mixture. Bake on greased cookie sheet for 15 minutes. Garnish with lemons and parsley. Yield: 12 servings

BLACK-EYED PEA DIP

3 (15-ounce) cans black-eyed peas, drained and rinsed
1 each: green and yellow bell pepper, chopped
1 small purple onion, chopped
1 medium tomato, seeded and chopped
¼ cup chopped cilantro
1 cup Italian dressing
½ teaspoon Worcestershire sauce
Several shakes of dried basil and oregano
Salt and pepper to taste

Combine all ingredients, and mix well. Chill overnight before serving. Serve with corn chips. Yield: 24 servings

CRUNCHY COLESLAW

¾ cup real bacon bits
2 cups shredded cabbage
4 tablespoons chopped green bell pepper
2 tablespoons lemon juice
½ cup mayonnaise
2 tablespoons chopped parsley
1 tablespoon grated onion
½ cup sesame seeds, toasted
1 cup sliced almonds, toasted

Combine bacon, cabbage, and pepper; set aside. Whisk together lemon juice, mayonnaise, parsley, and onion. Toss cabbage mixture with dressing. Top with sesame seeds and almonds. Yield: 8–10 servings

PEAR TART

TART SHELL

1¾ cups all-purpose flour
½ cup ground almonds
6 tablespoons sugar
1 stick frozen butter, cut into small pieces
1 egg

Mix flour, almonds, sugar, and butter in food processor. Slowly add egg. When dough forms a ball, remove dough. Wrap dough in wax paper; chill 30 minutes to one hour. Roll out on floured wax paper; press into 10-inch removable-bottom tart pan.

FILLING

½ cup sugar, divided
5 Bosc pears, peeled, cored, and halved
2 tablespoons butter, cut into pieces

Preheat oven to 375 degrees. Sprinkle 3 tablespoons sugar on crust. Slice pear halves horizontally from tip to stem end, keeping slices in place. Arrange pears fan-like with tip pointing toward center of circle. Sprinkle with remaining sugar, and dot with butter. Bake 40 minutes or until crust is light brown.

GLAZE

¼ cup red currant jelly
1 tablespoon sugar

In a saucepan, heat jelly and sugar over medium heat. Stir with wire whip 2 minutes or until jelly forms syrup. While Glaze is still warm, paint pears with a soft pastry brush. Yield: 16 servings

USE CACHEPOTS AS SERVING CONTAINERS
AND DECORATE THE PLATTERS WITH
NATIVE GREENERY.

WHITE WINE CAKE

½ cup finely chopped pecans
1 (18.25-ounce) box butter recipe golden cake mix
1 (3-ounce) package instant vanilla pudding
½ cup vegetable oil
4 large eggs, room temperature
½ cup white wine
½ cup water

Preheat oven to 325 degrees. Combine cake mix, pudding mix, oil, eggs, wine, and water with mixer and pour into Bundt pan that has been sprayed with cooking spray containing flour and sprinkled with pecans. Bake for 40–50 minutes or until toothpick comes out clean. Remove cake from oven and place in pan on wire rack. Pour Glaze over hot cake in pan, and allow to soak in for 15 minutes. Remove from pan. Yield: 16–20 servings

GLAZE

1 stick unsalted butter, melted
1 cup sugar
¼ cup white wine

Dissolve sugar in butter. Stir in wine.

Anniversary Dinner

A wedding anniversary is a very special time to celebrate love and family. It may be silver, golden, or any years in between. A traditional dinner around the family dining table serves much more than food for nourishment; it presents a true sense of the importance of family. It means belonging to one another. It means working, playing, and going through life with shared love and security. We thrive on traditions as we treasure stories of the past to create a bond with the present to pass on to future generations. Celebrate with a meal made from family recipes amid heirlooms and wedding gifts of the honored couple. Be sure to have albums and photographs to enjoy sharing stories and memories.

Great ideas

NAPKIN ETIQUETTE

Place your napkin in your lap, folded in half and opening forward, as soon as you are seated, except at a very formal dinner when you wait for the hostess to place her napkin in her lap. When the meal is finished, place your napkin to the left of your plate, but do not fold it.

As a general rule, dinner napkins are 20–26 inches square, luncheon napkins are 14–18 inches square, tea napkins are 10–12 inches square, and cocktail napkins are 4–6 inches square.

Napkins may be placed on the plate, between the plate and the charger, to the left of the silver in the place setting, or in glasses.

FAN FOLD

Fold the napkin in half, then pleat like a fan. Press the fan in half, and place it inside the glass. Add a few small flowers.

TULIP FOLD

Fold the napkin in half diagonally to form a triangle. Fold the sides up to the point forming a square. Fold the bottom point of square half way up. Place in the glass and pull down the center and the two sides.

FLOWER POCKET

Fold the napkin in half diagonally to form a triangle. Fold the bottom edge halfway upward to form a pocket. Turn the sides under and tuck a flower inside the pocket.

NAPKIN RING

Fold the napkin in quarters and slip into a napkin ring. Collect different silver antique napkin rings and give them to friends for gifts.

Menu

COQUILLES OF SHRIMP AND
LUMP CRABMEAT
STUFFED MUSHROOMS
GRAPEFRUIT AND AVOCADO SALAD
CORNISH HENS WITH WILD RICE
TOMATOES ROCKEFELLER
CARROT SOUFFLÉ
ICEBOX ROLLS
DIVINE CHOCOLATE CAKE
LEMON ANGEL FOOD ICEBOX CAKE

COQUILLES OF SHRIMP AND LUMP CRABMEAT

2 sticks butter
2 heaping tablespoons all-purpose flour
1 pint whipping cream
½ cup sherry
¼ cup chopped celery
1 tablespoon chopped parsley
Red pepper to taste
2 tablespoons Worcestershire sauce
2 cups mayonnaise
2 pounds lump crabmeat
1 pound shrimp, peeled, deveined, and cooked
1 cup crushed potato chips
½–¾ cup finely grated cheese

Preheat oven to 325 degrees. Melt butter; add flour and stir. Gradually add whipping cream, stirring continually. Stir in sherry, celery, parsley, red pepper, and Worcestershire; stir until thickened. Cool; stir in mayonnaise, crabmeat, and shrimp. Pour into buttered shells, ramekins, or casserole dish. Sprinkle potato chips and cheese on top. Bake for 25 minutes. Yield: 12 servings

STUFFED MUSHROOMS

1 pound fresh medium-sized mushrooms
¼ pound each: mild sausage and hot sausage, chopped
¼ cup grated Parmesan cheese

Preheat oven to 350 degrees. Clean mushrooms and remove stems. Combine sausages and place 1 teaspoon inside each mushroom. Sprinkle with cheese. Bake 25–30 minutes. Yield: 24 mushrooms

TOMATOES ROCKEFELLER

2 (10-ounce) packages frozen chopped spinach
1 cup soft bread crumbs
1 cup seasoned bread crumbs
1 cup chopped green onions
6 eggs, slightly beaten
¾ cup butter, melted
½ cup grated Parmesan cheese
½ teaspoon minced garlic
1 teaspoon thyme
Dash of Tabasco Sauce
12 thick tomato slices

Preheat oven to 350 degrees. Cook spinach according to package directions; drain and squeeze out water. Mix spinach with remaining ingredients, except tomatoes. Mound mixture on top of each tomato slice. Bake for 15 minutes. Yield: 12 servings

GRAPEFRUIT AND AVOCADO SALAD WITH CREAMY FRENCH DRESSING

3 grapefruits, peeled and sectioned
3 avocados, peeled, sliced, and sprinkled with lemon juice
Leaf lettuce
½ cup blue cheese, crumbled
½ cup toasted and coarsely chopped walnuts

Place 3 grapefruit sections and 3 avocado slices on a lettuce leaf and drizzle with dressing just before serving. Sprinkle with blue cheese and walnuts. Yield: 12 servings

CREAMY FRENCH DRESSING

½ tablespoons dry mustard
¾ tablespoon paprika
¾ tablespoon salt
¾ cup confectioners' sugar
2 cups oil
½ cup vinegar
1 egg, beaten
Juice of 1½ lemons and 1½ oranges
½ tablespoon Worcestershire sauce
½ clove garlic

Combine dry ingredients with oil, vinegar, and egg; beat vigorously. Add juices and Worcestershire. Put garlic in mixture for 1 hour; then remove. Shake before serving. Yield: 2¾ cups

CORNISH HENS STUFFED WITH WILD RICE

¼ cup chopped onion
2 tablespoons butter
½ cup wild rice, cooked
¼ cup slivered and toasted almonds
⅛ teaspoon each: salt, thyme, and marjoram
2 Cornish game hens
2 strips bacon

Preheat oven to 325 degrees. Sauté onion in butter. Combine rice, onions, almonds, spices, and mix well. Salt and pepper hens inside and out and stuff with rice mixture. Place a strip of bacon on top of each hen. Place in roaster, uncovered, and bake for 1½–2 hours; baste often. If not tender, cover and steam until done. Yield: 2 hens

CARROT SOUFFLÉ

2 pounds carrots, cooked
1 cup finely chopped celery
1 medium onion, finely chopped
3 or 4 green onions, tops and bottoms, chopped
1 tablespoon mustard
½ cup mayonnaise
1 cup crushed crackers
3 tablespoons butter

Preheat oven to 300 degrees. Mash cooked carrots. Add celery, onion, mustard, and mayonnaise. Place in a 9x13-inch dish; top with crackers and dot with butter. Bake for 1 hour. Yield: 8–10 servings

ICEBOX ROLLS

2 cups milk
⅔ cup sugar
⅔ cup shortening
1 package yeast
½ cup lukewarm water
4½ cups all-purpose flour, divided
1 teaspoon baking soda
1 teaspoon baking powder
2 teaspoons salt

Scald 2 cups milk. While hot, add sugar and shortening. Cool to lukewarm. Dissolve yeast in lukewarm water for 5 minutes. Pour yeast mixture into milk mixture. With mixer, beat 3 cups sifted flour into the milk to make a thin batter. Cover with cloth; set aside and allow to rise for 2 hours.

Sprinkle baking soda, baking powder, and salt on top of dough and beat into dough with a spoon. Add 1½ cups flour until you can handle like biscuits. Knead; chill at least 6–8 hours. (Dough will keep chilled for 1 week covered with foil and punched down.) Remove and roll out on a floured surface, cut with biscuit cutter, spread melted butter on tops, and fold over. Place on a lightly greased pan and let rise 2 hours in warm place. Bake in a 375-degree oven 15–20 minutes. Yield: 5 dozen rolls

DIVINE CHOCOLATE CAKE

1 (18.25-ounce) Devil's food cake moist pudding
    cake mix
1 (14-ounce) can sweetened condensed milk
1 (12.25-ounce) jar caramel topping
1 (8-ounce) container whipped topping
1 cup Heath bar bits

Bake cake in a 9x13-inch pan according to directions. Punch holes in warm cake with a straw. Pour condensed milk over cake. Pour caramel topping over cake. Cool and ice with whipped topping and sprinkle with Heath bits. Chill. Yield: 20 servings

LEMON ANGEL FOOD ICEBOX CAKE

6 eggs, separated
¾ cup sugar
½ cup lemon juice
1½ tablespoons grated lemon rind
1 tablespoon gelatin, soaked in ¼ cup water
Pinch of salt
⅔ cup sugar
1 large angel food cake, sliced into strips

Beat egg yolks with ¾ cup sugar, lemon juice, and rind. Heat in a double boiler until thick. While hot, mix in gelatin and water mixture; cool.

Beat egg whites until stiff; beat in salt and ⅔ cup sugar. Fold whites into cooled custard. Spray Bundt pan with cooking spray. Alternate cake strips and custard until mold is filled. Chill several hours or overnight.

Remove from refrigerator and dip mold in warm water. Turn cake out. Frost with Icing. Yield: 16 servings

ICING

1 pint whipping cream
2–4 tablespoons confectioners' sugar
For garnish: lemon slices and flowers

Beat whipping cream with mixer until soft peaks form, then beat in sugar. Ice cake and garnish with lemon slices and flowers.

Paris Chic Debutante Party

This fashionable party, with debutantes in mind, would also be a great tea reception for a bride, graduate, retiree, or birthday lady. Alert guests of the feminine fun that is in store with a shoe-shaped invitation announcing the event. Cover a straw hat with preserved hydrangea petals, and add a ribbon band and fresh flowers for the door. Greet guests in the entrance with a mirrored table displaying vintage brooches for each to select and enhance their present ensemble as well as wear home for a favor. The food table echoes the "lady" theme with an oversized hydrangea-covered, high-heeled shoe with a large, pink, silk organza bow filled with an assortment of pink flowers. The menu consists of an assortment of delicious pick-up treats. Punch is served from a collection of antique tea cups circling a large silver bowl with a few floating flowers. After visiting and sipping tea and posing for group photos in vintage furs and hats in front of a cheval mirror, the ladies exit a little more "chic" with a small bottle of Chanel perfume tied with a tag including some of Coco's quotes such as, "A woman who doesn't wear perfume has no future," or "Fashion passes, style remains," or "A woman can be over-dressed, never over-elegant," or "Luxury is when the inside is as beautiful as the outside."

Great ideas

IT'S A GIRL THING

Glue preserved hydrangea flowerettes to a straw hat for a door decoration. Guests may select a vintage brooch from a center table at the front entrance. Decorate a craft store dress form for a table decoration.

Collect vintage furs and hats in front of a cheval mirror for guests to model in group photographs.

For favors, give guests a small bottle of Chanel perfume with a tag highlighting favorite Coco quotes.

Menu

CALLA LILY SANDWICHES

BACON AND OLIVE SANDWICHES

CHICKEN SALAD IN CREAM CHEESE
    SHELLS

PARISIAN MACAROONS

CHERRY CREAM TARTS

LOU'S PETIT FOURS

PRALINES

CHOCOLATE TURTLES

CARAMELS

AMBER TEA PUNCH

CALLA LILY SANDWICHES

1 (2-ounce) package slivered almonds
3 drops yellow food coloring
54 slices white sandwich bread
1 (8-ounce) package cream cheese, softened
1 tablespoon orange marmalade

Combine almonds and food coloring in jar with lid; shake until almonds are yellow and set aside. Roll each slice of bread ⅛ inch thick and cut in circle with 2½-inch biscuit cutter. Combine cream cheese and marmalade. Spread 1 teaspoon cream cheese mixture on each bread round. Pinch lower edge of circle together to form the base of lily and press a yellow almond into the pinched portion as the stamen. Yield: 54 sandwiches

BACON AND OLIVE SANDWICHES

1 (8-ounce) package cream cheese, softened
2 tablespoons whipping cream
½ teaspoon white pepper
¼ cup bacon bits
3 tablespoons chopped stuffed green olives
3 tablespoons toasted and chopped walnuts
16 slices wheat bread
For garnish: mayonnaise and chopped parsley

Combine cream cheese, cream, and pepper; mix well. Stir in bacon, olives, and nuts. Spread on bread for sandwiches. Trim crusts and cut each into 3 fingers. Brush mayonnaise around edges and dip in parsley. Yield: 2 dozen sandwiches

CHICKEN SALAD IN CREAM CHEESE SHELLS

CREAM CHEESE SHELLS

½ cup butter, softened
1 (3-ounce) package cream cheese, softened
¼ teaspoon salt
¼ cup grated Parmesan cheese
1½ cups all-purpose flour

Preheat oven to 425 degrees. Beat together butter and cream cheese. Beat in salt and Parmesan cheese until well combined. Beat in flour, and knead dough into ball. Shape into 8-inch log; cut into 24 slices. On a lightly floured surface, roll each slice into a 3-inch circle and press into a miniature muffin cup. Bake for 5–7 minutes. Cool. Yield: 24 cups

CHICKEN SALAD

2 large chicken breasts, boiled and finely chopped
½ cup mayonnaise
1 teaspoon lemon juice
Salt, black pepper, and white pepper to taste
For garnish: sliced almonds and parsley

Combine chicken, mayonnaise, lemon juice, salt, and peppers. Spoon into shells and sprinkle with almonds and parsley.

Parisian Macaroons

6 ounces blanched almonds
1⅔ cup confectioners' sugar
3 large egg whites, room temperature
¼ teaspoon salt
3 tablespoons sugar
Food coloring

Preheat oven to 300 degrees. Pulse almonds in food processor until finely ground. Add confectioners' sugar to almonds and pulse until combined; set aside. Beat egg whites and salt with mixer until foamy and soft peaks form. Add sugar, a tablespoon at a time, beating after each. Add food coloring, if desired. Beat until stiff peaks form. Stir whites into almond mixture until incorporated. Transfer mixture to pastry bag with round tip #2A, and pipe 1½-inch circles on parchment-lined baking sheets. Let stand 5 minutes. Bake 11 minutes on top rack and 11 minutes on bottom rack. Cool for one hour on baking sheet placed on wire rack. Yield: 24 sandwich cookies

FILLING FOR PINK MACAROONS

½ (12-ounce) container buttercream icing
2 tablespoons strawberry or raspberry jam

Combine icing and jam. Spread onto half of macaroons and sandwich with remaining macaroons.

FILLING FOR GREEN MACAROONS

½ (12-ounce) container buttercream icing
1 teaspoon lime juice

Combine icing and lime juice. Spread onto half of macaroons and sandwich with remaining macaroons.

Cherry Cream Tarts

1 (8-ounce) package cream cheese, softened
1 (14-ounce) can sweetened condensed milk
⅓ cup lemon juice
1 teaspoon vanilla
3 (1.9-ounce) packages mini filo shells
1 (21-ounce) can cherry pie filling

Beat cream cheese with mixer until fluffy. Add condensed milk, lemon juice, and vanilla; beat until smooth. Spoon into shells and top with pie filling. Yield: 45 tarts

Lou's Petit Fours

CAKE

1 (18.25-ounce) package white cake mix
¼ teaspoon almond extract

Preheat oven to 350 degrees. Prepare mix according to package directions, and add almond extract. Pour into a greased 10½x15½-inch jellyroll pan. Bake 17–20 minutes; do not brown top. Remove to rack and immediately cover with wax paper; pat to adhere. In 5 minutes, pull off wax paper to remove crust. Cool; place new wax paper on cake. Place rack on wax paper and turn cake out. Brush crumbs from bottom. Freeze cake.

Remove cake and wax paper, and frost top with a thin layer of Buttercream Frosting. Trim ⅛ inch off edges with serrated knife and cut into 1½-inch squares. Then ice with Fondant Icing and decorate. Yield: 60 petit fours

BUTTERCREAM FROSTING

1 cup shortening, or ¾ cup Quick Blend shortening, room temperature
⅛ teaspoon salt
1 teaspoon Wilton butter flavoring
¼ teaspoon almond extract
1 (2-pound) bag confectioners' sugar

Beat shortening and salt until fluffy. Put flavorings in cup and add water to make ½ cup liquid. Add sugar and water mixture alternately to shortening while mixing. Will keep in refrigerator for 3 weeks.

FONDANT ICING

⅞ cup skim milk
3 tablespoons shortening or Quick Blend shortening
⅛ teaspoon salt
1½ teaspoon clear vanilla
1½ teaspoon Wilton butter flavoring
⅛ teaspoon almond extract
1 (2-pound) bag confectioners' sugar, sifted

In a double boiler, combine milk, shortening, and salt. Remove from heat. Never return to heat; thin with hot milk. Add vanilla, butter flavoring, and almond extract. Mix in sugar with hand mixer. Place rack over wax paper to catch drips. Pour ½ cup icing over each cake held with a spatula over icing. Remove excess icing and cool on rack. When set, decorate with Buttercream Frosting.

PRALINES

½ pint whipping cream
1 (1-pound) box light brown sugar
2 tablespoons margarine
2 cups pecans

Microwave whipping cream and sugar for 13 minutes on high. Stir in margarine and pecans. Stir until not shiny. Drop by teaspoonfuls on foil. Yield: 24 pieces

CHOCOLATE TURTLES

72 pecan halves
24 caramels, unwrapped
6 ounces almond bark
1 (6-ounce) bag semisweet chocolate chips

Preheat oven to 300 degrees. On a greased baking sheet, arrange pecan halves in groups of 3, end to end, flat sides down. Place a caramel on top of each cluster. Place in oven for 5 minutes. Remove and flatten caramel with a buttered spoon. Cool. Heat almond bark and chips in microwave on defrost at 2-minute intervals until melted. Dip turtles in chocolate to coat. Place on wax paper to cool. Yield: 24 pieces

CARAMELS

2 cups sugar
1 cup light corn syrup
3 (½-pint) containers whipping cream
2 cups chopped pecans

Heat sugar and corn syrup on medium heat for 7 minutes until it begins to turn yellow. Add cream, stirring constantly for 25 minutes until it reaches soft-ball stage on candy thermometer. Add pecans; pour into an buttered 11x15-inch pan. Cool; cut into 1-inch pieces and wrap by twos in wax paper. Yield: 160 pieces

AMBER TEA PUNCH

½ cup sugar
4 cups hot tea
24 ounces apricot nectar
½ cup lemon juice
2 cups orange juice
1 (28-ounce) bottle ginger ale, chilled

Dissolve sugar in tea. Add nectar and juices; chill. Add ginger ale. Yield: 1 gallon, 30 servings

USE A COLLECTION OF DIFFERENT ANTIQUE
TEA CUPS TO SERVE PUNCH. GARNISH
THE PUNCH WITH FLOWERS FLOATING IN
SMALL ICE RINGS.

Christmas Buffet

Christmas is a wonderful time to have a large party. It is a time to celebrate and extend love to all we hold dear. Everything is festive, and friends love a reason to slow down and share time with one another, especially over beautifully displayed food that is special and delicious. For a large buffet party, planning, preparation, and organization are key elements. The dining table keeps its formal theme by offering Pork Tenderloin with rolls and sauces, Baked Salmon, Sesame Chicken, and Cheese Muffins with Caviar on silver trays surrounding a large urn of pavé red roses flanked by topiaries placed on a plaid silk runner. The buffet, also decorated with roses, ribbons, and greenery, is the place to enjoy stacked trays of delightful sweets and a Cheesecake with Chocolate Ganache and Raspberry Sauce served from a gold, ruffled-edged cake stand. Cheeses, fruits, and a fig and pecan Gorgonzola Terrine are served from pottery among greenery in the sunroom. After guests enjoy this feast and fellowship, they are ready to begin the season with warm hearts.

Menu

Pork Tenderloin and Rolls
with Cranberry-Horseradish
Sauce and Aïoli
Baked Salmon with Dill Sauce
Sesame Chicken with Thai Sauce
Cheese Muffins with Caviar
Cheese Tray
Gorgonzola Terrine
Eggnog Logs
Cheesecake with Chocolate
Ganache and Raspberry Sauce

Pork Tenderloin

½ cup Worcestershire sauce

1 cup orange juice

1 teaspoon each: lemon pepper, garlic salt, and Tony
 Chachere's Creole seasoning

6–8 pork tenderloins (about 1 pound each)

Combine seasonings in a zipper bag. Marinate tenderloins in seasonings for 2 hours to overnight. Grill or
bake in oven at 350 degrees until meat thermometer
reads 170 degrees. Let rest 10 minutes; slice. Serve with
rolls. Yield: 80 or more servings

CRANBERRY-HORSERADISH SAUCE

1 (12-ounce) bag fresh cranberries

1 (5.25-ounce) jar horseradish

1 teaspoon dry mustard

1 (10-ounce) jar apple jelly

Cook cranberries as directed. Add horseradish,
mustard, and jelly. Chill. Yield: 2 cups

AÏOLI

1 cup oil, divided

1 egg

1½ teaspoons salt

Pepper to taste

4 cloves garlic, chopped

2 teaspoons lemon juice

In a blender, mix ¼ cup oil, egg, salt, pepper, garlic, and
lemon juice until smooth. Add remaining oil slowly.
Yield: 1½ cups

Baked Salmon

1 cup mayonnaise

3 green onions, minced

3 tablespoons each: chopped dill, parsley, basil, and
 thyme

4 tablespoons minced red bell pepper

Juice of 1 lemon

Salt, ground black pepper, and cayenne pepper

4–5 pound salmon fillet, skin intact

For garnish: lime slices and parsley

Preheat oven to 350 degrees. Combine all ingredients
except salmon. Spread mixture over salmon within ½
inch of the edge. Spray baking dish with nonstick spray
and warm in oven for 20 minutes. Place salmon skin side
down in dish; it will sizzle. Bake 25–30 minutes or until
flaky and skin is crispy. Skin may be eaten or removed.
Garnish with lime and parsley. Serve with Dill Sauce and
crackers or toast points. Yield: 24–30 servings

DILL SAUCE

1 cup fresh dill, loosely packed

¼ cup olive oil

1 tablespoon pine nuts

2 cloves garlic

¼ teaspoon white pepper

1 cup half-and-half

½ cup heavy whipping cream

1 cup grated Romano cheese

Process dill, olive oil, pine nuts, garlic, and pepper in
food processor; set aside. Bring half-and-half and cream
to a simmer. Whisk in dill mixture and cheese; heat until cheese melts. Yield: 4 cups

SESAME CHICKEN WITH THAI SAUCE

40 chicken tenders
½ cup honey
½ cup soy sauce
1 cup pineapple juice
2 cups all-purpose flour
2 cups panko (Japanese bread crumbs)
½ cup sesame seeds
2 tablespoons granulated garlic
⅛ cup dried ground ginger
2 tablespoons black pepper
1 tablespoon white pepper
1 teaspoon salt

Beat chicken tenders flat with a meat mallet; run a 10-inch skewer down the center of each. Place the skewers in a flat pan with honey, soy sauce, and juice and marinate for one hour. Combine flour, panko, sesame seeds, and seasonings. Remove each skewer of marinade-coated chicken from pan and coat in flour mixture, making sure to pat onto all sides of chicken. Deep-fry each skewer at 350 degrees for 3–4 minutes or until done. Serve with Thai Sauce for dipping. Yield: 40 servings

THAI SAUCE

¾ cup creamy peanut butter
¼ cup sesame oil
1 tablespoon–⅛ cup Thai chili paste
½ cup honey
⅓ cup soy sauce
¼ cup rice vinegar
1 teaspoon minced fresh garlic
1 teaspoon minced fresh ginger
⅛ cup chopped green onions
¼ cup chopped cilantro
2 tablespoons sesame seeds

Blend together peanut butter, oil, chili paste, honey, soy sauce, vinegar, garlic, and ginger. Stir in onions, cilantro, and sesame seeds. Yield: 2½ cups

CHEESE MUFFINS WITH CAVIAR

1 cup shredded sharp Cheddar cheese
2 sticks butter, softened
1 cup sour cream
2 cups self-rising flour
For garnish: sour cream, red or black caviar, and parsley

Preheat oven to 350 degrees. Blend cheese, butter, and sour cream in food processor. Transfer mixture to bowl; add flour. Spoon into lightly greased mini-muffin pans. Bake for 15–20 minutes. To serve, top each muffin with a dollop of sour cream, caviar, and parsley. Yield: 4 dozen muffins

GORGONZOLA TERRINE

½ cup chopped dried figs
4 or 5 sprigs fresh thyme
1 cup orange juice or red wine
1 pound cream cheese, softened
1½ sticks butter, softened
8 ounces Gorgonzola cheese, crumbled
1 teaspoon salt
1 cup toasted and chopped pecans, divided
2 tablespoons chopped parsley
For garnish: fresh figs and thyme

Simmer chopped figs with thyme and orange juice or wine over low heat for 15 minutes. Drain; discard thyme. Let cool. Mix cream cheese and butter. Add Gorgonzola and salt. Do not overmix. Line a loaf pan with plastic wrap. Spoon in ½ of cheese mixture. Scatter cooked figs, ½ cup pecans, and parsley over cheese mixture. Spoon remaining cheese mixture into pan, and cover with plastic wrap. Give pan a few sharp raps to settle terrine and refrigerate. To remove terrine from pan, turn upside down on a flat surface. Pull off plastic wrap. Garnish with remaining ½ cup pecans, fresh figs, and thyme. Serve with crackers. Yield: 25–30 servings

EGGNOG LOGS

1 cup butter, softened
¾ cup sugar
1 large egg
2 teaspoons vanilla
1 teaspoon rum flavoring
3 cups all-purpose flour
1 teaspoon nutmeg
1 (12-ounce) can vanilla frosting, softened
1 cup finely chopped pecans

Preheat oven to 350 degrees. Beat butter and sugar with mixer; add egg, vanilla, and rum flavoring. In a separate bowl, combine flour and nutmeg. Add to butter mixture, mixing well. Divide dough into 10 portions. Roll each portion out into a 12-inch pencil-shaped log; cut log into 3-inch logs. Bake for 10–12 minutes. When cool, dip each end into vanilla frosting, and roll in pecans. Yield: 4–5 dozen logs

CHEESECAKE WITH CHOCOLATE GANACHE AND RASPBERRY SAUCE

1 envelope unflavored gelatin
⅔ cup water
2 (8-ounce) packages cream cheese, softened
2 cups semisweet chocolate morsels, melted
1 (14-ounce) can sweetened condensed milk
1 cup heavy cream, whipped
Anna's Ginger Thins

Sprinkle gelatin over water in a saucepan. Heat, stirring, until dissolved; set aside. Beat cream cheese and melted chocolate in a bowl until fluffy. Add condensed milk. Stir into dissolved gelatin. Fold in whipped cream. Pour into a bowl, and refrigerate for 3 hours or overnight.

Unmold onto a platter, and cover with Chocolate Ganache. Garnish with Raspberry Sauce. Serve with Anna's Ginger Thins. Yield: 24–30 servings

CHOCOLATE GANACHE

1 cup heavy cream
8 ounces bittersweet chocolate

Heat cream in a saucepan until it comes to a boil. Remove from heat; add chocolate, and stir well to combine. Let cool, and pour over cake.

RASPBERRY SAUCE

2 cups raspberries
¼ cup sugar
2 tablespoons Grand Marnier liqueur

Blend all ingredients in a blender. Strain and chill until ready to serve.

FOR A CHEESE TRAY, SERVE SEVERAL VARIETIES OF SOFT AND HARD CHEESES, MILD AND SHARP CHEESES, SOME FRESH FRUIT, A HONEY COMB, AND SOME TOASTED NUTS WITH A VARIETY OF CRACKERS.

Formal Holiday Dinner

A formal dinner with close friends is a treasured gift of time, talents, and effort. Successful entertaining presents an inviting atmosphere for guests as they enjoy delicious food and each other's company. Organization and advanced planning are essential. From invitations to decorations, the minute one enters the front door, the stage is set for a delightful evening with the beautifully set dining table. Topiaries in rustic urns among cones, shiny Christmas balls, and elegant flowers and berries are juxtaposed with several compatible antique china patterns and silver goblets. This elegant event is executed in five courses beginning with Roasted Red Bell Pepper Soup and ending with Caramel Custard with mint and berries. The entire evening is truly a beautiful gift to all.

Menu

ROASTED RED BELL PEPPER SOUP
WITH CHEESE CRACKERS

MIXED GREEN SALAD WITH BALSAMIC
VINAIGRETTE AND BRUSCHETTA
WITH GOAT CHEESE AND PARSLEY

RASPBERRY SORBET

PEPPER-COATED STEAK WITH BRANDY
AND CREAM

DUCHESS POTATOES

HERB BAKED TOMATOES

CARAMEL CUSTARD

ROASTED RED BELL PEPPER SOUP

3 red bell peppers
¾ cup chopped onion
3 cloves garlic, chopped
1 stick unsalted butter
2½ cups chicken broth
1 tablespoon chopped parsley
l teaspoon dried thyme
Salt and pepper to taste
For garnish: Crème Fraiche or sour cream,
    Johnny-Jump-Ups, bell pepper curls

Place bell peppers on the rack of broiler pan 4–6 inches under the broiling element. Keep the oven door ajar. Turn to blacken evenly on all sides. When peppers are blackened on all sides, remove from heat and immediately place in a sealed zipper bag. Allow steaming in the bag until cool. Peel, seed, and chop.

Sauté onion and garlic in butter for 10 minutes. Add bell peppers and sauté an additional 10 minutes. Add chicken broth, parsley, and thyme. Simmer, uncovered, 20 minutes. Season with salt and pepper. Cool; purée in food processor or blender. If soup is too thick, thin with additional broth. Top with Crème Fraiche and serve with Cheese Crackers. Yield: 8 servings

CRÈME FRAICHE

1 cup whipping cream
1 cup sour cream

Whisk cream and sour cream. Cover loosely with plastic wrap and chill at least 4 hours. (May store in refrigerator up to 2 weeks.) Pour Crème Fraiche in plastic squeeze bottle and make decorative designs on top of soup. Yield: 2 cups

CHEESE CRACKERS

2 sticks margarine, softened
1 cup shredded sharp Cheddar cheese
2 cups all-purpose flour
2 cups Rice Krispies
1 teaspoon red pepper
½ teaspoon salt

Cream margarine and cheese; add remaining ingredients and mix well. Roll into 2 or 3 logs 1½ inches in diameter; chill until firm. Slice and bake at 350 degrees for 12–15 minutes. Freezes well, or may be stored in sealed tin for 2–3 weeks. Yield: 5 dozen crackers

MIXED GREEN SALAD WITH BALSAMIC VINAIGRETTE

4 cups mixed field greens
1 cup toasted and coarsely chopped walnuts
Whole fresh strawberries, fanned
Balsamic vinaigrette

Toss lettuce, walnuts, and strawberries. Add dressing; toss, and serve immediately. Yield: 8 servings

CRISPY BRUSCHETTA WITH GOAT CHEESE AND PARSLEY

1 baguette, cut into 12 (½-inch thick) slices
3 tablespoons olive oil
1 garlic clove, halved
4 ounces goat cheese, plain or herb
3 tablespoons chopped parsley

Preheat oven to 325 degrees. Arrange bread slices on baking sheet. Brush olive oil over both sides of bread. Bake bread 6 minutes per side. Remove; rub cut sides of garlic over toasts. Toasts may be made one day ahead and stored in airtight container at room temperature.

Preheat oven to 350 degrees. Spread baguettes with goat cheese. Arrange on baking sheet and bake 5 minutes. Garnish with parsley. Yield: 12 servings

RASPBERRY SORBET

2 pints fresh or frozen raspberries
¼ cup sugar
1 teaspoon balsamic vinegar
1 teaspoon fresh lemon juice
2 tablespoons Kirsh

Purée berries, sugar, vinegar, and lemon juice in blender or food processor until smooth. Sieve mixture to remove seeds. Add Kirsh. Add more sugar, if needed, for desired sweetness. Pour into a freezer tray; freeze until about one inch of the mixture is frozen on all sides of the tray. Remove and beat mixture with mixer until mushy. Return to tray and freeze until firm. Yield: 8 small servings

PEPPER-COATED STEAK WITH BRANDY AND CREAM SAUCE

8 slices thin white bread
8 (8-ounce) filets, 1½ inches thick, trim fat and tie around with twine
4–6 tablespoons black peppercorns, crushed
4 tablespoons oil
½ cup brandy

Cut bread rounds the size of steaks. Toast on both sides; cool and place on serving plates. Dip both sides of filet into pepper and press so some will stick. Heat oil until it begins to smoke. Place fillets in pan and lower heat to medium. Cook to desired doneness, 3 minutes each side for rare and 4 minutes each side for medium. Salt only after turning. Place over toast and keep warm. Remove excess peppercorns from steak pan and add brandy. Heat and flame. Stir to deglaze pan and reduce to half. Add brandy mixture to heated Cream Sauce. Taste for seasoning. Pour Cream Sauce plus brandy mixture over filets; serve immediately. Yield: 8 servings

CREAM SAUCE

1 pint heavy cream
1 teaspoon Bovril
1 tablespoon lemon juice
½ teaspoon salt
3 tablespoons Madeira wine

Heat cream over high heat, whisking frequently until reduced to half and thickened; set aside. Combine Bovril, lemon juice, salt, and Madeira, and bring to a boil. Add to reduced cream. This can be done the day before. Chill. Bring to room temperature before reheating. In saucepan, reheat reserved sauce to just before boiling. Whisk constantly. It could curdle if it boils.

LARGE FLORAL ARRANGEMENTS ARE IDEAL ON SERVING TABLES, WHILE SMALLER SCALE CENTERPIECES ARE MORE DESIRABLE AT SEATED TABLES TO AVOID INTERRUPTING CONVERSATION.

DUCHESS POTATOES

2 cups mashed potatoes
3 egg yolks
3 tablespoons butter, softened
2–3 tablespoons heavy cream
Freshly ground pepper and salt to taste

Preheat oven to 400 degrees. Beat potatoes with mixer. Add yolks, butter, cream, pepper, and salt. Transfer to a pastry bag and pipe while warm into individual mounds onto cookie sheet. Drizzle each mound with melted butter. Bake for 20–30 minutes. Yield: 8 servings

HERB BAKED TOMATOES

4 tomatoes
Salt to taste
2 tablespoons olive oil
1 teaspoon dried thyme
1 teaspoon dried basil
Salt and pepper to taste
½ cup stale bread crumbs
3 garlic cloves, minced
¼ cup minced parsley
Salt and pepper to taste

Preheat oven to 400 degrees. Half and core tomatoes. Remove seeds, sprinkle with salt, and invert on rack to drain for 20 minutes. Place tomatoes right side up in an oiled dish. Sprinkle with olive oil, thyme, basil, salt, and pepper. Bake for 10 minutes. Combine bread crumbs, garlic, parsley, salt, and pepper. Divide among tomatoes. Drizzle pan juices on tomatoes. Bake for 10 minutes. Place under broiler 2–3 minutes or until tops are lightly browned. Yield: 8 servings

A WATER BATH OR BAIN MARIE IS A METHOD OF GENTLY COOKING CUSTARDS AND MOUSSES TO KEEP THEM FROM BREAKING OR CURDLING. THE CONTAINERS OF FOOD ARE PLACED IN A SHALLOW PAN OF WARM WATER FOR BAKING.

CARAMEL CUSTARD

⅓ cup sugar
2 tablespoons water
2½ cups milk
½ cup sugar
4 eggs, beaten
1 teaspoon vanilla
For garnish: berries, orange slices, and mint

Preheat oven to 350 degrees. Bring ⅓ cup sugar and water to a boil, making sure the sugar is dissolved. Turn heat to high and heat to amber color. Coat 6 custard molds with caramel. Heat milk and ½ cup sugar; stir until sugar dissolves. Cool slightly. Slowly pour warm milk mixture into beaten eggs. Add vanilla. Strain custard into caramel-lined molds. Place molds in a water bath by placing molds in a pan and pouring boiling water around molds to come halfway up the sides. Bake 40 minutes until custard is set or until knife plunged through the center of custard comes out clean. Chill. To unmold, run knife around edge of mold. Place serving dish over mold, reverse, and remove the mold from custard. Garnish with berries, orange slices, and mint. Yield: 8 servings

Victorian Valentine Brunch

Send lacy, feminine valentines for invitations and invite some special girlfriends for a Victorian brunch. Set the table, as the Victorians would have, with beautiful hand-painted china and polished silver and an abundance of multi-colored flowers and fruits flowing from antique lusters with prisms. The meal, especially for ladies, consists of quiche, salads, and muffins with a delicious over-the-top Chocolate Marble Cheesecake for dessert. For a Valentine favor, send each friend home with a small Victorian plate of homemade chocolates.

Menu

CRABMEAT QUICHE
MINTED FRUIT SALAD
BROCCOLI SALAD
BACON WRAPS
BLUEBERRY MUFFINS
PECAN PIE MUFFINS
CHOCOLATE MARBLE CHEESECAKE

CRABMEAT QUICHE

½ cup mayonnaise
2 tablespoons flour
½ cup milk
3 eggs, beaten
Salt, black pepper, and white pepper to taste
½ teaspoon nutmeg
1 cup shredded Swiss cheese
1 (6-ounce) can crabmeat, cleaned and picked
¼ cup chopped green onions
1 (9-inch) unbaked pie shell

Preheat oven to 350 degrees. Blend mayonnaise, flour, milk, eggs, salt, peppers, and nutmeg. Stir in crabmeat, cheese, and onions. Spoon into the pie shell. Bake 40–45 minutes. Yield: 6 servings

MINTED FRUIT SALAD

Cantaloupe, honeydew, pineapple pieces, strawberries, and grapes

MINT DRESSING

1 tablespoon Dijon mustard
1 tablespoon sherry vinegar
1 tablespoon honey
¼ cup chopped mint
¼ cup orange juice

Whisk Mint Dressing ingredients together, pour over fruit pieces, and mix well. Chill. Yield: 10–12 servings

BROCCOLI SALAD

1 cup mayonnaise
¼ cup sugar
1 tablespoon white wine vinegar
2 bunches broccoli, cut and soaked 2 hours in cold water
½ cup raisins
½ cup pecans
⅓ cup bacon bits
2 green onions, chopped

Mix mayonnaise, sugar, and vinegar together. Drain broccoli, and toss with raisins, pecans, bacon bits, and green onions. Toss with dressing. Yield: 8–10 servings

BACON WRAPS

8 slices bread
1 (14-ounce) can sweetened condensed milk
1 tablespoon Worcestershire sauce
1 teaspoon dry mustard
2 cups shredded Cheddar cheese
1 (12-ounce) package bacon

Cut crust from bread and flatten with rolling pin. Combine condensed milk, Worcestershire, and mustard. Spread a spoonful of mixture on bread and sprinkle with cheese. Roll up with a slice of bacon; toothpick together. Cut in half and bake at 350 degrees for 10–15 minutes in a pan with sides. Yield: 16 pieces

BLUEBERRY MUFFINS

1¼ cups all-purpose flour
1 cup sugar
2 teaspoons baking powder
¼ teaspoon salt
1 teaspoon cinnamon
2 eggs, beaten
4 tablespoons butter, melted
1 cup milk
1 teaspoon vanilla
⅛ teaspoon lemon extract
½ teaspoon lemon zest
1 cup fresh blueberries, dusted in small amount of flour

Preheat oven to 400 degrees. Grease 2 miniature muffins pans. Combine flour, sugar, baking powder, salt, and cinnamon; set aside. Beat eggs, and stir in butter, milk, vanilla, lemon extract, and zest. Make a well in dry ingredients; pour in egg mixture. Stir until flour is moistened. Fold in blueberries. Spoon batter into muffin tins, filling ⅔ full. Bake for 20–25 minutes. Allow to sit for 5 minutes before transferring to a wire rack to cool. Yield: 24 miniature muffins

DUST BERRIES IN FLOUR TO KEEP THEM
FROM SINKING TO THE BOTTOM OR
CLUMPING TOGETHER IN MUFFINS OR CAKES.

PECAN PIE MUFFINS

1 cup chopped pecans
1 cup brown sugar, firmly packed
½ cup all-purpose flour
½ cup butter, melted
2 eggs, beaten

Preheat oven to 350 degrees. Combine pecans, sugar, and flour; set aside. Add butter to eggs, and then add to dry ingredients, stirring until moistened. Spray miniature muffin pans with nonstick cooking spray; spoon batter into cups, filling each cup ⅔ full. Bake for 14–16 minutes. Remove from pans immediately, and cool on wire racks. Yield: 24 miniature muffins

CHOCOLATE MARBLE CHEESECAKE

3 (8-ounce) and 1 (3-ounce) packages cream cheese, softened
1¼ cups sugar
3 tablespoons cake flour
¼ cup heavy whipping cream
½ tablespoon vanilla
4 eggs
2 tablespoons cocoa
For garnish: strawberries and 8-ounce chocolate bar, melted

Preheat oven to 300 degrees. Line 9-inch springform pan with parchment and coat sides with butter; set aside. Beat cream cheese with mixer until creamy. Combine sugar and flour and add to cream cheese. Add cream and vanilla. Stir in eggs; do not mix or cake will crack. Remove 1½ cups of batter and mix in cocoa. Pour half of plain batter into pan. Pour in cocoa batter. Pour in remaining half of plain batter. Marbleize by making a figure 8 pattern with a knife. Place in oven on a cookie sheet and turn to 250 degrees. Bake 50 minutes; turn oven off and leave cake in oven for 30 minutes. Remove and cool to room temperature. Chill. Place strawberries on cake and drizzle with melted chocolate bar. Yield: 12–16 servings

Wedding Celebrations

Marry Me Dinner

The marriage proposal is a very special moment that the bride and groom will remember forever. This simple dinner, prepared by the future groom or the couple together, can be a memory to repeat on every anniversary. The menu of green salad, Char-Grilled Filet Mignon, Twice Baked Potatoes, and Sour Cream Biscuits is easy to prepare, delicious, and special. For dessert, Brownie and Oreo Tuffles can be easily prepared ahead of time and placed on a special plate. Then for that special evening, the truffles are placed on an elegant plate along with the proposal written in chocolate and a chocolate arrow holding the engagement ring. Don't forget an orchid or plant for the table and lots of flowers for the new fiancé.

Menu

CHAR-GRILLED FILET MIGNON

TWICE BAKED POTATOES

GREEN SALAD WITH RED WINE
    DRESSING

SOUR CREAM BISCUITS

OREO AND BROWNIE TRUFFLES WITH
    CHOCOLATE HEARTS AND ARROWS

CHAR-GRILLED FILET MIGNON

2 (8-ounce) filet mignons, wrapped in bacon
    (1½–2 inches thick)
Salt and pepper to taste
4 tablespoons unsalted butter
⅛–¼ cup Worcestershire Sauce
½ teaspoon Italian seasoning
¼ teaspoon coarsely cracked black pepper
¼ teaspoon garlic salt
¼ teaspoon onion powder

Sprinkle filets liberally with salt and pepper, pressing lightly to coat. For sauce, mix remaining ingredients together. Heat ½ of sauce in a small pan and reduce by ½ over low heat; set aside. Marinate steaks in ¼ of remaining sauce for 3–4 hours. Bring filets to room temperature and discard marinade. Prepare fire in charcoal grill. Grill steaks over hot coals for 8–10 minutes per side (5 minutes per side for rare). Baste steaks frequently with remaining ¼ of sauce on each side while cooking. For perfect steaks, turn them only once. Drizzle reduced sauce over hot steaks and let sit 5 minutes before cutting. Yield: 2 servings

TO REDUCE A SAUCE, BOIL RAPIDLY SO THAT
SOME OF THE LIQUID WILL EVAPORATE
LEAVING A THICKER CONSISTENCY AND A
MORE INTENSE FLAVOR.

TWICE BAKED POTATOES

1 large baking potato
4 tablespoons butter, divided
3 green onions, white parts only, chopped
⅓ cup half-and-half
¼ cup bacon bits
½ cup shredded Cheddar cheese, divided
½ teaspoon salt
½ teaspoon pepper

Preheat oven to 450 degrees. Wrap potato in aluminum foil and bake for 1 hour. Allow to cool until able to touch. Lower oven temperature to 350 degrees.

Sauté green onions in 2 tablespoons butter until soft. Cut the potato in half lengthwise. Carefully scoop out the pulp, leaving ¼ inch margin around the skins. Place the pulp in bowl. Mix the potato pulp with half-and-half, remaining butter, green onions, bacon bits, salt, pepper, and ½ of cheese. Fill potato skins with the mixture and place on greased baking pan. Bake for 20–25 minutes. During last 5 minutes of baking, sprinkle with remaining cheese. Yield: 2 servings

Green Salad with Red Wine Dressing

1 tablespoon Dijon mustard
1 tablespoon red wine vinegar
¼ cup olive oil
2 cups spring mix with herbs

Mix Dijon mustard and red wine vinegar in a large bowl. Whisk in olive oil until desired consistency is obtained. Drizzle over salad mix and toss to coat. Yield: 2 servings

Sour Cream Biscuits

1 stick butter, melted
1 tablespoon buttermilk
1 (8-ounce) carton sour cream
2 cups biscuit mix

Preheat oven to 425 degrees. Grease miniature muffin tins. Combine ingredients and blend thoroughly with a fork. Drop into miniature muffin cups and bake 12 minutes. Yield: 2½–3 dozen miniature biscuits

Truffles

OREO TRUFFLES

½ (1 pound, 2-ounce) package Oreo cookies, crushed
½ (8-ounce) package cream cheese, softened
½ (24-ounce) package vanilla or chocolate almond bark
For garnish: gold dust, jimmies, or cocoa (optional)

Combine crushed cookies and cream cheese. Roll into balls and refrigerate until hard. Melt almond bark in a glass bowl in the microwave at 2-minute intervals on defrost until melted (3–4 minutes). Dip each ball into almond bark with a toothpick and allow to harden on wax paper. If desired, sprinkle with gold dust, jimmies, or cocoa. Yield: 20 truffles

BROWNIE TRUFFLES

1 (19.8-ounce) package brownie mix, prepared and
baked according to package directions
1 (7-ounce) can milk chocolate icing
¼ cup sugar
Mini chocolate chips, chopped pecans, toasted and
chopped almonds, or powdered cocoa

Frost brownies with icing. Cut into squares and dip bottoms in granulated sugar. Cut each brownie into fourths and roll into 1-inch balls. Roll balls in mini chocolate chips, pecans, toasted almonds, or cocoa. Will keep in refrigerator about 2 weeks, or about 2 months in the freezer. Yield: 36 truffles

CHOCOLATE HEARTS OR ARROWS

1 cup semisweet chocolate chips
1 teaspoon shortening

Add a special touch to your dessert plate with chocolate hearts or arrows. Place a piece of wax paper on a cookie sheet and draw the desired shape with a pencil. Melt chips and shortening in a microwave dish at 2-minute intervals on defrost until melted. Pour mixture into a squeeze bottle with tip. Pipe hearts or arrows on wax paper and refrigerate until hardened. When hardened, lace the ring onto the arrow and transfer to plate with truffles. Then, write the question in chocolate onto a plate and sprinkle the plate with gold dust.

Meet the Family

After the ring is on the finger, the parents and families need to get to know their future in-laws. According to *Emily Post's Etiquette*, the parents of the groom should make the first move to become acquainted with the bride's family. The parents and couple will have many things to discuss with one another about the upcoming wedding, from locations of events to the guest list. This beautiful table and delicious dinner will make the meeting of family members a memorable occasion. The center of the dining table is lined with low, clear vases filled with an array of white flowers with a bird of paradise in each to add color and interest. Each vase sparkles with a simple gold leaf square that has been glued to the side with adhesive size. Golden napkin rings are simple wooden curtain rings that have been gold leafed. The meal, which consists of a simple Caesar Salad, Pork Medallions with Dried Cranberries over pasta, Asparagus with Brie Sauce, and a refreshing strawberry dessert that is easily prepared ahead of time, is a great beginning for the very special reason of its occurrence.

Menu

CAESAR SALAD
PORK MEDALLIONS WITH DRIED
    CRANBERRIES OVER VERMICELLI
ASPARAGUS WITH BRIE SAUCE
BETSY'S FROSTED STRAWBERRY
    SQUARES

CAESAR SALAD

1 bag romaine lettuce
1 bag mixed salad greens
1 (20-ounce) bottle Cardini's Original Caesar Dressing
Parmesan cheese, finely grated

Combine salad greens. Add dressing, and sprinkle with cheese. Yield: 6–8 servings

PORK MEDALLIONS WITH DRIED CRANBERRIES

1½ pounds boneless pork tenderloins, cut into ¾-inch slices
Salt and pepper to taste
2 tablespoons olive oil
2 tablespoons butter
All-purpose flour
1 clove garlic, minced
½ cup chopped green onions
1½ cups chicken broth
1 tablespoon Creole mustard
2 tablespoons maple syrup
1 cup dried cranberries

Season pork with salt and pepper. Heat oil and butter in large skillet. Flour pork lightly, and sauté until brown. Remove meat from pan. Add garlic and onions to skillet, and sauté. Whisk in chicken broth and mustard, and bring to a boil. Boil for 5 minutes to reduce slightly. Add syrup and cranberries. Bring to a boil, then add pork medallions. Cook until pork is completely done. Serve over vermicelli. Yield: 6 servings

ASPARAGUS WITH BRIE SAUCE

1 pound fresh asparagus
3 tablespoons butter
2 tablespoons all-purpose flour
1½ cups milk
8 ounces Brie cheese
Salt and pepper to taste

Steam asparagus until spears change color but are crisp. For sauce, melt butter in saucepan over moderate heat. Whisk in flour and cook about 2 minutes. Slowly whisk in milk, and bring to a boil, stirring frequently. Cut rindless Brie into small pieces, and add to the sauce. Stir until melted. Season with salt and pepper. Spoon sauce over cooked asparagus, and serve immediately; sauce thickens as it cools. Yield: 6 servings

BETSY'S FROSTED STRAWBERRY SQUARES

1 cup all-purpose flour
¼ cup brown sugar
½ cup chopped nuts
½ cup margarine, melted

Preheat oven to 350 degrees. Stir together all ingredients, and spread in a 9x13-inch pan. Bake for about 20 minutes. Remove from oven, and stir with a spoon several times to make crumbs. Allow to cool.

FILLING

2 egg whites
⅔ cup sugar
1 (10-ounce) package frozen strawberries, thawed and undrained
2 tablespoons lemon juice
1 cup whipped topping

Combine egg whites, sugar, strawberries, and lemon juice; beat with mixer on high speed for 10–15 minutes. Fold in whipped topping. Spread Filling over crumbs and freeze. Yield: 15–18 squares

Will You Be My Bridesmaid?

Being asked to be a matron or maid of honor or a bridesmaid for a dear friend is certainly a special honor. It might be fun to ask your friends to be your bridesmaids with a surprise luncheon, including some wedding details. The light and refreshing meal has its setting under the trees, complete with a chandelier, and is themed with shells and pearls. A matelasse bedspread covers the table, set with simple straw mats and tasteful china that was actually purchased from discount stores. White lilies, terracotta roses, and Queen Ann's Lace spill from a center urn. Smaller arrangements in shell containers with printed cards asking, "Will you be my bridesmaid?" are placed at each setting. A delicious salad plate is followed by a decadent dessert served with coffee, hot tea, or cappuccino. And each bridesmaid leaves with a shell vase or jewelry holder made by securing a pearlescent nautilus shell to a small painted, wooden trapezoid base with a small screw. This might also be the perfect time for mom and dad to surprise the bride with a small Bible, an heirloom lace handkerchief, and family jewelry, maybe even with something blue, for the wedding.

Great ideas

Send each bridesmaid home with a shell vase remembrance made by securing a pearlescent nautilus shell to a painted, wooden base. Add a strand of pearls for the upcoming parties.

In keeping with "Something old, something new, something borrowed, and something blue," mom and dad might surprise their daughter with an heirloom lace handkerchief, a small Bible, mom's wedding pearls, and a sapphire ring.

RESPONSIBILITIES OF BRIDESMAIDS AND THE MATRON OR MAID OF HONOR

Bridesmaids and the matron or maid of honor should help the bride with tasks to prepare for the wedding and give her love and support at all times.

They must each purchase a bridesmaid's dress and shoes.

They should help give a bridal shower or bridesmaids' brunch or luncheon.

They should attend as many parties prior to the wedding as possible.

They should attend the bridesmaids' brunch or luncheon.

They should attend the rehearsal and the rehearsal dinner.

They should be in the group to catch the bridal bouquet unless they are married.

They should remain at the reception until the bride and groom leave for the honeymoon.

RESPONSIBILITIES OF THE MATRON OR MAID OF HONOR AT THE WEDDING

During the wedding, the matron or maid of honor is responsible for having the groom's ring, holding the bridal bouquet when the couple exchanges vows, and for arranging the bride's train and veil when she arrives at the altar.

Menu

SHRIMP RÉMOULADE OVER SPRING SALAD GREENS
TOMATO ASPIC
DEVILED EGGS
ASPARAGUS SANDWICHES
EGGNOG CAKE

SHRIMP RÉMOULADE OVER SPRING SALAD GREENS

2 bags spring salad greens mix

BOILED SHRIMP

2 tablespoons salt
1 bag Zatarain's crab boil
1 lemon, quartered
Cayenne pepper to taste
3 quarts water
4 pounds fresh shrimp

Add salt, crab boil, lemon pieces, and pepper to boiling water in a large pot. Bring to a rolling boil. Add shrimp. Bring to a boil. Boil for one minute, cut off heat, and leave shrimp in water for 15 minutes. Peel and devein shrimp. Chill. Yield: 8 servings

RÉMOULADE SAUCE

½ cup Duke's mayonnaise
2½ tablespoons Zatarain's Creole mustard
4 teaspoons horseradish
4 teaspoons lemon juice, or to taste

Mix all ingredients together.

TO ASSEMBLE

Place salad greens on plate, top with shrimp, and spoon on Rémoulade Sauce.

TOMATO ASPIC

1 (.25-ounce) package gelatin
½ cup plus 1 teaspoon cold water
2 cups tomato juice, heated
2 tablespoons lemon juice
½ teaspoon salt
⅛ teaspoon white pepper
1 tablespoon onion juice
3 drops Tabasco Sauce
½ cup finely chopped celery
½ cup sliced stuffed olives
2 teaspoons sugar
For garnish: leaf lettuce, mayonnaise, and paprika

Dissolve gelatin in ½ cup plus 1 teaspoon cold water; add to heated tomato juice. Stir in remaining ingredients. Pour into oiled individual molds or Bundt pan; chill. Remove from mold by placing bottom of mold in warm water. Place on lettuce leaf; add a dollop of mayonnaise with a dash of paprika. Yield: 12–16 servings

DEVILED EGGS

12 hard-cooked eggs
⅓ cup mayonnaise
2 tablespoons sweet pickle relish
1½ teaspoons Durkee's Famous Sauce
Salt and pepper to taste
For garnish: paprika

Slice eggs lengthwise, remove yolks, and set aside whites. Place yolks in a bowl. Add mayonnaise, pickle relish, Durkee's sauce, salt, and pepper. Press gently together with a fork. Mound the mixture into the egg whites. Spinkle with paprika. Yield: 24 servings

ASPARAGUS SANDWICHES

1 (14-ounce) can asparagus, drained
1 (8-ounce) package cream cheese, softened
1 teaspoon seasoning salt
Lemon juice to taste
1 loaf Pepperidge Farm thin-sliced bread
Parmesan cheese, grated
1 stick butter, melted
For garnish: red bell pepper strips

Combine asparagus, cream cheese, salt, and lemon juice in food processor. Spread mixture on slice of bread and top with a second slice. Cut crust edges from sandwiches. Using a pastry brush, brush both sides of sandwich with melted butter; sprinkle with Parmesan cheese. Toast on both sides at 400 degrees. Cut each sandwich into 2 triangles. Yield: 13 sandwiches

PLACE SANDWICHES ON PLATES TO RESEMBLE BUTTERFLIES BY PLACING TRIANGLE POINTS TOGETHER FOR WINGS AND ADDING A STRIP OF BELL PEPPER IN THE MIDDLE FOR THEIR BODIES.

EGGNOG CAKE

2 sticks butter, softened
1 (1-pound) box confectioners' sugar
5 eggs, separated and beaten
6 tablespoons bourbon
1 cup chopped pecans
2–3 dozen ladyfingers
½ pint whipping cream, whipped
For garnish: caramel sauce, fresh raspberries, and mint

Cream butter and sugar; set aside. Combine beaten egg yolks and bourbon, which cooks the yolks. Let sit for 5 minutes. Stir into creamed mixture. Beat egg whites until stiff peaks form. Fold beaten egg whites into creamed mixture and set aside. Line 9x13-inch pan with wax paper on bottom and sides. Line with ladyfingers, brown side down. Spread filling over ladyfingers. Place ladyfingers on top, brown side up. Spread with whipped cream. Can make one thick layer or several thin layers. Cover tightly with plastic wrap so ladyfingers will not dry out. Refrigerate at least 2 hours before serving. Cut into squares. Drizzle plate with caramel sauce. Place a square on top of sauce, and garnish with raspberries and mint. Yield: 12–16 servings

Engagement Announcement

The wedding date is set, the plans are progressing, and now, it is time to announce the engagement to the extended family and friends. And what better way than a lovely party with lots of special pick-up foods and lavish desserts, where everyone can mingle, visit, and get to know one another? This menu includes a variety of favorites. Many recipes can be prepared ahead of time and frozen, and others may be purchased or catered. Engagement parties usually have many hosts and hostesses so that all can share their specialties, from invitations and food to flowers and clean-up, making it easier and less expensive for all involved. The table decorations are all white flowers—roses, tulips, hydrangeas, lisianthus, azaleas, and Gerbera daises placed in silver vases and pitchers. As food is served at stations in different rooms of the house, guests may leisurely serve themselves. This party will be remembered and enjoyed by the honored bride and groom and their families, as well as all who contribute to the planning and preparation and all who attend. What a wonderful prologue for the wedding to follow!

Menu

Beef Brisket on rolls with Horseradish Mayonnaise

Seafood Dip

Tomato Appetizers

Swiss Cheese and Bacon Dip

Asparagus Tea Sandwiches

Cucumber Rounds

Fruit and Cinnamon Dip

Coconut, Lemon, and Caramel Tarts

Sandies

Chocolate Squares

Mini Vanilla Cupcakes

Tiramisù Bites

Almond Tea

Beef Brisket

1 (5- to 6-pound) beef brisket
1 tablespoon celery salt
1 tablespoon onion salt
1 (4-ounce) bottle liquid smoke
2 tablespoons Worcestershire sauce
1½ cups barbecue sauce

Place brisket in glass baking dish. Season with salts and liquid smoke; cover with plastic wrap and marinate for 4 hours to overnight. Remove plastic and add Worcestershire. Cover with foil and bake for 3–4 hours at 275 degrees. Cool, remove fat, and slice. Add barbecue sauce. Cover with foil and return to oven for one hour. Yield: 36–40 servings

HORSERADISH MAYONNAISE

1 cup mayonnaise
2 tablespoons prepared horseradish
1 teaspoon Worcestershire sauce
½ teaspoon red pepper

Combine and serve with brisket. Yield: 1¼ cups

Seafood Dip

1 (8-ounce) package cream cheese, softened
¼ cup mayonnaise
2 tablespoons milk
3 green onions, sliced
1 teaspoon Worcestershire sauce
2 tablespoons fresh lemon juice
½ teaspoon garlic salt
1¼ cups freshly grated Parmesan cheese, divided
6 ounces lump crabmeat
½ pound small shrimp, cooked and peeled
For garnish: fresh parsley

Preheat oven to 350 degrees. Combine all ingredients except seafood and ¼ cup cheese. Gently fold in seafood. Pour into a greased 1½-quart baking dish and sprinkle with remaining ¼ cup cheese. Bake for 20–30 minutes. Sprinkle with chopped parsley; serve with toast points or crackers. Yield: 20–24 servings

Tomato Appetizers

1 (15-ounce) package rolled pie crusts, thawed
Olive oil
1 cup blue cheese, crumbled
1 cup mayonnaise
2 tablespoons white wine vinegar
1 teaspoon dry mustard
2 tablespoons olive oil
¼ cup chopped basil
1 cup sliced and drained grape tomatoes

Preheat oven to 350 degrees. Cut flower shapes from crusts; lightly coat both sides with olive oil and bake on parchment-lined baking sheet for 10 minutes. Mix cheese, mayonnaise, vinegar, and mustard. Combine olive oil and basil. Put a teaspoon of cheese mixture on cracker, then ½ teaspoon basil mixture, and top with tomato. Bake 5 minutes. Yield: 50 appetizers

ALWAYS DRAIN SLICED TOMATOES ON PAPER TOWELS BEFORE USING FOR SANDWICHES OR APPETIZERS.

Swiss Cheese and Bacon Dip

1 (8-ounce) package cream cheese, softened
½ cup mayonnaise
4 ounces shredded Swiss cheese
2 green onions, chopped
1 (2.8-ounce) package real bacon bits
1 tablespoon lemon juice

Preheat oven to 350 degrees. Mix all ingredients until blended. Pour into a greased 1½-quart baking dish; bake for 10–15 minutes. Serve with corn chips. Yield: 20–24 servings

Asparagus Tea Sandwiches

1 pound asparagus, tough ends removed
¼ teaspoon salt
2 tablespoons butter, softened
¼ cup mayonnaise
1 teaspoon Dijon mustard
16 slices thin white bread

Fill saucepan with water; bring to a boil over high heat. Add asparagus and salt; blanch for 2 minutes and remove to ice water. Drain on paper towels and set aside. Combine butter, mayonnaise, and mustard. Spread mixture on one side of each slice of bread. Layer one of the slices with asparagus; place other slice on top. Trim crusts and cut into finger sandwiches. Cover with a damp paper towel until ready to serve. Yield: 2 dozen sandwiches

Cucumber Rounds

2 cucumbers, thinly sliced and drained
1 (8-ounce) package cream cheese, softened
2 ounces goat cheese
¼ teaspoon each: dill, thyme, basil, salt, and white pepper
½ stick butter
2 loaves thin-sliced white bread
For garnish: fresh dill

Cut bread into rounds with a cookie cutter and spread each with butter. Mix cream cheese, goat cheese, and spices. Spread on rounds. Top with cucumber slice and dill. Yield: 60 sandwiches

Fruit and Cinnamon Dip

Assorted fresh fruit
1 (6-ounce) carton vanilla yogurt
1 (3-ounce) package cream cheese, softened
½ teaspoon cinnamon

Beat cream cheese until creamy. Stir in yogurt and cinnamon. Serve with fruit. Yield: 1¼ cups

Coconut Tarts

1¾ cups milk
⅔ cup plus ½ cup sugar, divided
3 egg yolks, beaten
2 tablespoons all-purpose flour
2 tablespoons butter, melted
½ teaspoon vanilla
1 package gelatin, dissolved in ¼ cup cold water
3 egg whites
2 (1.9-ounce) packages mini filo shells
Whipped topping

Combine milk, ⅔ cup sugar, yolks, flour, butter, and vanilla in top of double boiler. Simmer until custard coats spoon. Pour small amount of custard into dissolved gelatin; then pour gelatin into hot custard. Stir until smooth. Cool in refrigerator. Beat egg whites and ½ cup sugar until stiff. Fold egg whites into custard. Spoon into filo shells and top with whipped topping. Yield: 30 tarts

LEMON TARTS

1 (14-ounce) can sweetened condensed milk
2 egg yolks
⅓ cup lemon juice
2 (1.9-ounce) packages mini filo shells
Whipped topping
For garnish: lemon zest

Stir condensed milk, yolks, and lemon juice together until blended. Chill and spoon into mini filo shells. Top with whipped topping and lemon zest. Yield: 30 tarts

CARAMEL TARTS

1½ cups sugar, divided
2½ cups milk, divided
1 stick margarine
½ cup sugar
4 egg yolks
4 tablespoons cornstarch
2 (1.9-ounce) packages mini filo shells
Whipped topping

Bring 1 cup sugar, 2 cups milk, and margarine to boil in saucepan. Caramelize remaining ½ cup sugar in separate saucepan over low heat. Slowly whisk caramelized sugar into boiling milk mixture. Combine egg yolks, cornstarch, and remaining ½ cup cold milk. Temper yolk mixture by adding a tablespoon of hot mixture and stirring. Then add egg mixture to hot mixture; stir until thick. Pour into filo shells and top with whipped topping. Yield: 30 tarts

SANDIES

1 pound butter, softened
1 cup confectioners' sugar, plus some for dusting
2 teaspooons vanilla
4 cups sifted all-purpose flour
3 cups chopped pecans

Preheat oven to 350 degrees. Cream butter and sugar with mixer. Add vanilla. Beat in flour and pecans. Form into mounds with spoon and bake on ungreased baking sheet for 10 minutes until lightly brown. Cool and sprinkle with additional confectioners' sugar. Yield: 75 cookies

CHOCOLATE SQUARES

¼ cup butter, softened
½ cup sugar
1 egg
1 (1-ounce) square unsweetened chocolate, melted
½ cup all-purpose flour

Preheat oven to 350 degrees. Cream butter and sugar; add egg. Add melted chocolate and flour. Pour into a greased 9x9-inch pan. Bake 11 minutes. Cool, frost, and glaze. Yield: 16 squares

FROSTING

2 tablespoons butter
1 cup confectioners' sugar
1 tablespoon cream
½ teaspoon vanilla

Mix well; chill 10 minutes, then spread on cooled cookie layer.

GLAZE

2 (1-ounce) squares unsweetened chocolate
2 tablespoons butter
For garnish: sliced almonds

Melt chocolate and butter. Pour over Frosting layer to form solid chocolate on top. Garnish with sliced almonds, and chill.

Mini Vanilla Cupcakes

3 cups cake flour
1 tablespoon baking powder
1 teaspoon salt
1¾ cups sugar
½ cup shortening
2 eggs
1 cup milk
1 teaspoon vanilla

Preheat oven to 350 degrees. Sift flour, baking powder, and salt together. Cream sugar and shortening. Add eggs, milk, and vanilla. Add flour mixture and combine. Pour into greased mini muffin tins and bake 10–12 minutes. Frost with Vanilla Frosting. Yield: 48 cupcakes

VANILLA FROSTING

2 sticks unsalted butter, softened
7–8 cups confectioners' sugar, divided
½ cup milk
1½ teaspoons vanilla
Food coloring (optional)

Beat butter and ½ the confectioners' sugar with mixer until creamy. Add milk and vanilla. Continue to beat at medium speed until smooth, 3–5 minutes. Add food coloring, if desired. Gradually add the remaining sugar, 1 cup at a time, beating 2 minutes after each addition until Frosting is of good spreading consistency. Spread or pipe onto cupcakes.

Tiramisù Bites

1 (18.25-ounce) package yellow cake mix
½ cup brewed coffee, cooled
1 (8-ounce) package cream cheese, softened
2 (3-ounce) packages vanilla instant pudding
3 cups milk
1 (8-ounce) container whipped topping, divided
For garnish: cocoa and 1 (1.55-ounce) Hershey bar,
    grated

Preheat oven to 350 degrees. Prepare mix according to package directions, and bake in greased mini muffin tins for 10–12 minutes. Place pan on wire rack. Punch holes into each cupcake with toothpick and drizzle with ½ teaspoon coffee. Remove from pans. Beat cream cheese until creamy; beat in pudding mixes and milk. Fold in half of whipped topping. Cut off top half of each cupcake; spread cream cheese mixture on bottom half. Place top on cupcake and freeze. Remove from freezer; spread with whipped topping and sprinkle with cocoa and chocolate. Yield: 48 bites

Almond Tea

1 gallon sweet tea
3 teaspoons almond flavoring
1 (6-ounce) can frozen lemonade, thawed
For garnish: fresh mint and lemon slices

Mix all ingredients together and garnish with mint and lemon slices. Yield: 1 gallon

Couples' Dinner Shower

A wedding shower is a gathering of family and friends in honor of an engaged couple. The name comes from a "showering" of gifts for the honored guest or guests. Wedding showers are usually held two weeks to two months before the wedding. They may be given by anyone who wants to honor the bride and groom. A couples' shower can be particularly enjoyable because the groom is included in the party and gets to share in opening the gifts. This dinner for close friends celebrates the bride and groom with a delicious seafood lasagna meal, which begins with Bacon-Tomato and Blue Cheese-Walnut Tartlets for appetizers and ends with a White Chocolate Macadamia Nut Key Lime Pie for dessert. The types of showers for couples are endless. Themes can be miscellaneous, round-the-clock, or entertainment showers with gifts such as board games, movies with popcorn, a picnic basket, or tickets to plays, concerts, museums, or sporting events. Showers for gardening equipment, kitchen gadgets, Christmas ornaments, and favorite books provide needed items for the new household. A couples' shower could lead to the formation of a supper club that will meet and enjoy one another for years to come.

Menu

Bacon-Tomato and Blue Cheese-Walnut Tartlets

Layered Spinach Salad with Creamy Horseradish Dressing

Shrimp and Scallop Lasagna

Garlic Cheese Biscuits

White Chocolate Macadamia Nut Key Lime Pie

Bacon-Tomato and Blue Cheese-Walnut Tartlets

1 (12-ounce) can Hungary Jack buttermilk biscuits

Preheat oven to 350 degrees. Split each biscuit into three pieces. Press dough into mini-muffin tins. Top with filling of choice, and bake 10–12 minutes. Yield: 36 tartlets

BACON-TOMATO FILLING

6 slices bacon, cooked, drained, and crumbled
  (or prepared bacon bits)
1 medium tomato, seeded and chopped
3 ounces grated mozzarella cheese
½ cup Hellmann's mayonnaise
1 teaspoon Italian seasoning
¾ teaspoon garlic salt

Mix together all ingredients; stir well.

BLUE-CHEESE WALNUT FILLING

6 slices bacon, cooked, drained, and crumbled
  (or prepared bacon bits)
4 ounces blue cheese
¼ cup chopped walnuts
3 green onions, chopped
½ cup Hellmann's mayonnaise

Mix together all ingredients; stir well.

Layered Spinach Salad with Creamy Horseradish Dressing

½ pound fresh spinach
½ pound bacon, fried and crumbled
5 hard-boiled eggs, chopped
1 head lettuce, torn
1 package frozen peas, uncooked but thawed
1 onion, chopped
¼ pound shredded Swiss and Cheddar cheese
Sugar, salt, and pepper to taste
For garnish: cheese, bacon bits, and slivered almonds

Layer first 7 ingredients in order. Sprinkle with sugar, salt, and pepper. Top with Dressing. Garnish with more cheese, bacon, and slivered almonds. Chill until ready to serve. Yield: 12–16 servings

DRESSING

1 cup mayonnaise
1 cup sour cream
3 teaspoons horseradish
1 (1-ounce) package dry ranch dressing mix

Mix together all ingredients.

Shrimp and Scallop Lasagna

12 lasagna noodles
3 tablespoons unsalted butter
1 small onion, finely chopped
2 cloves garlic, minced
3 tablespoons all-purpose flour
2½ cups half-and-half
1 cup grated Romano cheese
½ teaspoon salt
¼ teaspoon pepper
¾ pound sea scallops, cut in half or quartered, if large
¾ pound medium shrimp, peeled and deveined
½ cup grated Parmesan cheese

Preheat oven to 375 degrees. Spray a 10x13-inch baking dish with vegetable oil cooking spray. In a large pot of boiling salted water, cook lasagna noodles for about 8 minutes. Drain and set aside. Melt butter in heavy skillet; cook onion over low heat for about 5 minutes or until soft. Add garlic and cook for 1 minute. Increase heat to medium-low; stir in flour with a whisk. Gradually add half-and-half, allowing sauce to thicken slightly. When sauce is consistency of whipping cream, add Romano and stir well. Add salt and pepper; set aside. Sauté scallops for 3–4 minutes. Add shrimp, and cook for 1–2 minutes or until they turn pink. Turn off heat. Spoon about 2 tablespoons of sauce into the prepared dish. Cover bottom with 4 noodles, placing them side by side. Spoon ⅓ of sauce over noodles and top with seafood. Repeat with noodles and remaining sauce. For the top layer, spoon only sauce over noodles. Tuck in edges of noodles and coat with sauce. Top with Parmesan. Bake for 20–25 minutes, uncovered, until bubbly. Allow to sit for 10 minutes before slicing. Yield: 12 servings

GARLIC CHEESE BISCUITS

1¼ cups biscuit mix
½ cup grated sharp Cheddar cheese
½ cup water

Preheat oven to 400 degrees. Line baking sheet with parchment paper. Combine biscuit mix and cheese. Add water, and stir just until combined. Dough will be slightly moist. Drop by tablespoonfuls onto the prepared baking sheet. Bake for 10 minutes or until biscuits are firm and beginning to brown. While biscuits are baking, make Garlic Butter. Remove biscuits from oven; brush with Garlic Butter using a pastry brush. Yield: 12 biscuits

GARLIC BUTTER

½ stick unsalted butter, melted
¼ teaspoons garlic powder
¼ teaspoon salt
⅛ teaspoon parsley flakes

Combine all ingredients; mix well.

IT MIGHT BE FUN TO GIVE THE BRIDE AND GROOM MATCHING APRONS WITH THE RECIPES FROM THE SHOWER IN THE POCKETS AS GIFTS.

WHITE CHOCOLATE MACADAMIA NUT KEY LIME PIE

CRUST

½ cup chopped macadamia nuts
1 deep-dish graham cracker crust
4 ounces white chocolate
8 tablespoons butter, cubed

Sprinkle nuts in bottom of crust. Melt chocolate and butter; pour over nuts and freeze.

FILLING

4 egg yolks
1 (14-ounce) can sweetened condensed milk
½ teaspoon grated lime peel
6 ounces Key lime juice

Preheat oven to 350 degrees. Whisk egg yolks, condensed milk, and lime peel. Gradually stir in lime juice. Pour into frozen crust and bake 20 minutes. Let cool.

TOPPING

1 (8-ounce) carton heavy cream
1 tablespoon sugar
For garnish: Key lime slices

Whip cream with sugar and spoon on top of cooled pie. Garnish with lime slices. Yield: 6–8 servings

Doves and Birdcages

Love doves inside golden birdcages with shades of pink roses, lacy filler, green hydrangeas, and white dendrobian orchid garlands strung on fishing line display a romantic theme for this tea shower. A birdcage with flowers and a small nest of eggs greets guests at the front door, and another calls attention to the guest register, while others of all sizes and shapes, spilling with flowers, decorate seating tables where guests may enjoy leisurely visiting over tea, coffee, sandwiches, and dainty desserts. It is polite to send gifts ahead of time to a large shower, allowing the hostess time to attractively and orderly display them for all to view. Assign one hostess the job of photographer to snap photos of the bride, her mother, and future mother-in-law visiting with friends and family during the party. Don't forget pictures of the hostesses, the tables of decorations and food, and the gift display. These can be presented to the bride in a small album as a remembrance of the day. Continuing the theme, the hostesses could give the bride a birdcage filled with pretty stationery, pens, and desk supplies, an antique birdcage music box, or a small pair of love doves as a personal gift.

Great ideas

Begin the theme at the front door with a birdcage filled with flowers and a small nest of eggs.

Place a bird cage on the table where guests sign the guest register.

Create a small photo album of the shower as a gift to the bride from the hostesses.

A painted birdcage filled with stationery and desk supplies with the bride's new initials makes a great gift for the bride.

An antique birdcage music box gift would be a special memory of the shower.

CHICKEN SALAD SANDWICHES

2 chicken breasts, cooked and finely chopped
½ cup toasted and finely chopped pecans
½ cup sweetened dried cranberries
1 teaspoon lemon juice
1 teaspoon finely grated orange peel
Black pepper and white pepper to taste
½ cup mayonnaise
1 loaf wheat bread, thinly sliced

Toast pecans in a 350-degree oven for 8–10 minutes and chop. Combine chicken, pecans, cranberries, lemon juice, orange peel, peppers, and mayonnaise. Spread between 2 slices of bread, remove crust, and cut into triangles. Yield: 20 sandwiches

ROMA TOMATO SANDWICHES

6 Roma tomatoes, sliced and drained
2 (8-ounce) packages cream cheese, softened
1 (1-ounce) package dry ranch dressing mix
½ cup feta cheese, crumbled
¼ cup real bacon bits
2 loaves thinly sliced white bread
Salt and pepper to taste
For garnish: fresh basil

Slice tomatoes, and set aside on paper towels to drain. Combine cream cheese and dressing mix until well blended. Gently stir in feta and bacon bits. Cut bread slices into rounds or shape with a cookie cutter. Spread cream cheese mixture on each bread round, and top with a tomato slice. Sprinkle with salt and pepper, and garnish with basil. Yield: 30–40 sandwiches

CUCUMBER CREAM CHEESE HEARTS

1 cucumber, thinly sliced
1 loaf white bread, thinly sliced
1 (16-ounce) bottle cucumber ranch dressing
½ stick butter, softened
1 (8-ounce) tub cream cheese with chives and onions, softened
White pepper, paprika, and fresh parsley for garnish

Slice cucumber into thin slices; marinate in dressing for 1–2 hours, and drain on paper towels. Cut bread into small hearts with a cookie cutter. Spread bread with layer of butter, then cream cheese. Place a cucumber on each heart and sprinkle with white pepper and paprika and garnish with parsley. Store in an airtight container layered with damp paper towels in the refrigerator. Yield: 20 sandwiches

SWEET DIP

1 (8-ounce) package cream cheese, softened
½ cup sour cream
1 tablespoon sugar
¼ cup brown sugar
½ teaspoon cinnamon
1 teaspoon vanilla

Combine all ingredients with mixer until smooth. Serve with fresh seasonal fruit. Yield: 1½ cups

CINNAMON SUGAR PECANS

1 egg white
1 tablespoon water
1 pound pecans halves
1 cup sugar
1 teaspoon salt
1 teaspoon cinnamon

Beat egg white and water until frothy. Fold in pecans. Mix sugar, salt, and cinnamon in plastic zipper bag. Add pecans and shake until coated. Bake 30 minutes at 300 degrees, stirring 3 or 4 times. Pour on wax paper and separate while warm. Yield: 1 pound

BRIE AND CHUTNEY CUPS

1 (8-ounce) wheel Brie cheese, rind removed
2 sheets frozen puff pastry, thawed at room temperature
½ cup chopped walnuts
2 tablespoons butter
Cranberry hot pepper jelly

Preheat oven to 400 degrees. Cut cheese into 36 one-inch cubes and freeze. Sauté walnuts in butter, and set aside. Unfold puff pastry and cut out 36 rounds with a 2½-inch biscuit cutter; place each into cup of mini muffin pans that have been sprayed with nonstick cooking spray. Bake 5 minutes. Remove from oven, and place one Brie cube into each pastry shell. Bake 10 minutes or until edges are golden. Remove from pan and top with walnuts and ½ teaspoon pepper jelly. Yield: 36 cups

STRAWBERRY CUPCAKES

1 (18.25-ounce) box white cake mix
1 (3-ounce) package strawberry gelatin
1 cup oil
½ cup milk
4 eggs
1 cup frozen strawberries, thawed and drained
1 cup finely chopped pecans
1 cup grated coconut

Preheat oven to 350 degrees. Mix all ingredients well, and pour into mini muffin pans with liners. Fill about ⅔ full. Bake for 8–10 minutes. Cool and frost with Strawberry Icing. Yield: 36–40 cupckaes

STRAWBERRY ICING

1 stick margarine, softened
1 (8-ounce) package cream cheese, softened
1 pound confectioners' sugar
1 teaspoon vanilla
½ cup frozen strawberries, thawed and drained
½ cup finely chopped pecans
½ cup grated coconut

Beat margarine and cream cheese until smooth. Add sugar, vanilla, and strawberries, and mix well. Stir in pecans and coconut.

LEMON CUPCAKES

¼ cup butter, softened
¾ cup sugar
2 eggs
½ cup heavy cream
¼ cup fresh lemon juice
1 cup all-purpose flour
2 teaspoons baking powder
¼ teaspoon salt

Preheat oven to 350 degrees. Prepare mini muffin pans with liners. Cream butter and sugar and add eggs. Whisk in cream and lemon juice. Combine flour, baking powder, and salt. Stir dry mixture into creamed mixture. Spoon into muffin tins and bake for 10–12 minutes. Cool on wire rack. Pour Glaze over cooled cupcakes. Yield: 24 cupcakes

GLAZE

¾ cup confectioners' sugar
1 tablespoon fresh lemon juice
2 tablespoons lemon yogurt

Mix ingredients with whisk until smooth.

MELTING MOMENTS

1 cup butter, softened
⅓ cup confectioners' sugar
¾ cup cornstarch
1 cup all-purpose flour

Preheat oven to 350 degrees. Cream butter and sugar with mixer. Add cornstarch and flour. Cover and chill. Form into 1-inch balls and place on ungreased baking sheet. Press an indention with thumb into center of each ball. Bake 10–12 minutes; do not brown. Cool and spoon Frosting into indention. Yield: 24 cookies

FROSTING

1 (3-ounce) package cream cheese, softened
1 cup confectioners' sugar
1 teaspoon vanilla

Cream ingredients with mixer.

CREAM CHEESE MINTS

1 (3-ounce) package cream cheese, softened
2½ cups confectioners' sugar
2–3 drops peppermint flavoring
Food coloring (optional)
Sugar

Combine cream cheese and confectioners' sugar with mixer. Add flavoring and coloring, if desired. Roll into a small balls; roll balls in sugar and press into mold. Remove and chill until serving. Yield: 40 mints

APPLE MINT JULEPS

1 cup fresh mint, chopped
12 cups apple juice
½ cup fresh lime juice
For garnish: mint, sliced Key limes, orchids

Boil mint and apple juice; cool and refrigerate 3–4 hours. Pour juice through strainer and discard mint. Stir in lime juice. Serve over crushed ice. Garnish with mint, limes, and orchids. Yield: 16 servings

FLAVORED COFFEE

1 teaspoon ground cinnamon
1 teaspoon almond flavoring

Sprinkle cinnamon and almond flavoring into the dry coffee before brewing. Yield: 24–36 cups

Hen Party

This "hen party" shower is all about nesting. Everyone will enjoy a light plate of chicken salad, mixed greens, and fresh fruit with asparagus sandwiches and a time to visit with friends. Dessert is a choice of a delicious Chocolate-Walnut Pie or a refreshing Lemon Dessert with berries. Tables are set with colorful spring flowers and draped with feather boas with hand-painted, pottery birds perched above each plate. Gifts for the bride are things to help "feather her nest." This shower could be a linen shower with gifts for the bed and bath or a kitchen shower with gifts of kitchen items, favorite recipes, and a special apron signed with names and advice of all the guests. Whatever the case, the bride will leave with many items for her new nest from her favorite group of hens.

Menu

CHICKEN SALAD WITH PECANS
AND BACON

SPRING MIX SALAD WITH SWEET
PAPRIKA VINAIGRETTE

SEASONAL FRUIT WITH ORANGE
DRESSING

SESAME ASPARAGUS ROLL-UPS

LEMON DESSERT

CHOCOLATE-WALNUT PIE

CHICKEN SALAD WITH PECANS AND BACON

1 tablespoon lemon juice
1 cup mayonnaise
4 cups cooked and chopped chicken breasts
1 cup diced celery
1 cup toasted and chopped pecans
½ cup sweetened dried cranberries
Salt, black pepper, and white pepper to taste
1 (3-ounce) package bacon bits

Combine lemon juice and mayonnaise; blend well. Add chicken, celery, pecans, cranberries, and seasoning. Serve on lettuce leaf, and sprinkle with bacon bits. Yield: 8 servings

TO BOIL CHICKEN, PLACE A FEW STALKS
CELERY WITH LEAVES, HALF OF AN ONION,
AND 1 TEASPOON OF SALT IN A STOCKPOT
OF WATER. BRING TO A ROLLING BOIL,
ADD CHICKEN, AND BOIL FOR 5 MINUTES.
COVER POT, TURN OFF THE HEAT, AND
LET IT STAND FOR 20 MINUTES.

SPRING MIX SALAD WITH SWEET PAPRIKA VINAIGRETTE

½ stick butter
1 cup chopped walnuts
1 (3-ounce) package ramen noodles, crushed (discard flavor packet)
1 bag spring mix salad greens
½ cup dried cranberries
1 Granny Smith apple, sliced

Melt butter; add nuts and ramen noodles, and cook over low heat until lightly toasted; set aside. Place greens on plate; top with cranberries, apples, and nut mixture. Drizzle with Sweet Paprika Vinaigrette just before serving. Yield: 6–8 servings

SWEET PAPRIKA VINAIGRETTE

2½ tablespoons cider vinegar
2½ teaspoons honey
½ teaspoon lemon juice
½ teaspoon paprika
⅓ cup sugar
½ teaspoon dry mustard
½ teaspoon celery seed
½ teaspoon dried onion
½ cup vegetable oil

Mix all ingredients, except oil, in a pint jar. Heat in microwave for 30 seconds. Add oil and shake well. Vinaigrette may be made ahead and refrigerated; warm in microwave for 30 seconds when ready to serve. Yield: 6–8 servings

Seasonal Fruit with Orange Dressing

Fresh melon, grapes, strawberries, pineapple, kiwis, and grated coconut

ORANGE DRESSING

½ cup whipping cream
1 (6-ounce) can orange juice concentrate, thawed

Place in a fruit jar with lid and shake. Drizzle over fruit and sprinkle with coconut. Yield: 1¼ cups

Sesame Asparagus Roll-Ups

12 fresh asparagus spears
12 slices white bread, with crusts removed
½ cup blue cheese, crumbled
1 (8-ounce) package cream cheese, softened
1 stick butter, melted
1 tablespoon sesame seeds

Preheat oven to 375 degrees. Trim each asparagus spear to 6 inches long. Flatten bread between wax paper with a rolling pin. Mix blue cheese and cream cheese together, and spread on bread. Place an asparagus spear on each piece of bread; roll up. Dip each sandwich in melted butter. Place on an ungreased baking sheet, and sprinkle with sesame seeds. Bake 15 minutes or until golden. Yield: 12 sandwiches

Lemon Dessert

6 lemons, halved and juiced
1 (14-ounce) can sweetened condensed milk
½ cup fresh lemon juice
1 (8-ounce) container whipped topping
For garnish: berries, mint, and gingersnap crumbs

Level each lemon half by cutting small section off bottom. Blend condensed milk and juice. Fold in whipped topping. Spoon into lemons. Garnish with berries, mint, and cookie crumbs. Yield: 12 servings

Chocolate-Walnut Pie

1 (9-inch) pie shell, baked
1 cup sugar
¼ cup water
1¼ cups whipping cream, divided
8 ounces semisweet chocolate, cut into pieces
2 tablespoons butter
2 teaspoons vanilla
1¾ cups toasted and coarsely chopped walnuts, divided

After baking, cool pie shell on a wire rack 15 minutes. In a heavy saucepan, heat sugar and water over medium heat until sugar dissolves and turns amber (15 minutes, swirling pan occasionally). Heat ¾ cup cream in microwave on high for 45 seconds or until warm. Place remaining ½ cup cream in refrigerator. Remove saucepan from heat and stir in warm cream until a smooth caramel forms (will stiffen when cream is added). Stir in chocolate and butter until melted. Stir in vanilla and 1½ cups walnuts. Pour warm filling into shell. Cool one hour on wire rack, then cover and refrigerate 3 hours or until set. When ready to serve, in medium bowl, with mixer on medium speed, beat remaining ½ cup cream until soft peaks form. Spread whipped cream on top of pie. Sprinkle with reserved walnuts. Yield: 12 servings

WHIP CREAM IN A COLD BOWL
WITH COLD BEATERS.

Nuts and Bolts Shower

This shower is just for the guys. It begins with a spicy salsa served with chips. Appetizers are followed by a Mexican fiesta of Chicken Enchiladas over Confetti Rice with Fiesta Corn in a bell pepper and an avocado salad. The tables feature simple green plants with small hand tools, such as pliers, tape measurers, rulers, and levels attached with twine. Each place is set with a Mexican placemat topped with a square woven charger and a colorful fiesta plate. In keeping with the theme, napkins are tied with twine and accented with a hammer-shaped sugar cookie. As dessert plates of cookies and brownies are passed, the prospective groom opens tools that he will need for repairs and projects as he enjoys conversation with the friends that will help with his new tasks.

Menu

SALSA AND TORTILLA CHIPS
AVOCADO WITH MANDARIN ORANGES
CHICKEN ENCHILADAS
CONFETTI RICE
FIESTA CORN
CRANBERRY-NUT COOKIES
CHOCOLATE CHIP COOKIES
KAHLÚA BROWNIES

SALSA AND TORTILLA CHIPS

2 (14.5-ounce) cans diced tomatoes
2 (4-ounce) cans sliced black olives, drained
1 (4-ounce) can chopped green chiles, drained
4 green onions, green and white parts, chopped
1 (1-ounce) package Good Seasons salad mix, prepared according to package directions
¼ cup chopped fresh basil
1 (8-ounce) package Mexican cheese, shredded

Combine tomatoes, olives, chiles, onions, prepared salad mix, and basil; cover and chill. Stir in cheese just before serving. Serve with chips. Yield: 12–16 servings

AVOCADO WITH MANDARIN ORANGES

3 small avocados, peeled and sliced
1 head Bibb lettuce
2 (11-ounce) cans mandarin oranges

Cut avocados into 4 pieces; place on lettuce and top with oranges. Drizzle with Dressing. Yield: 6 servings

DRESSING

⅓ cup olive oil
⅓ cup wine vinegar
¼ teaspoon each: basil, salt, and black pepper

Combine ingredients in a jar; shake.

CHICKEN ENCHILADAS

1 small onion, chopped
1 tablespoon margarine
1 (4-ounce) can chopped green chiles, drained
1 (4-ounce) can chopped mushrooms, drained
1 (8-ounce) package cream cheese, softened and cut into small pieces
1 (10.75-ounce) can cream of chicken soup
3½ cups cooked, chopped chicken breasts
12 (8-inch) flour tortillas
1 (8-ounce) package shredded Monterey Jack cheese
1½ cups whipping cream

Preheat oven to 350 degrees. Sauté onion in margarine. Add chiles; sauté one minute. Stir in mushrooms, cream cheese, soup, and chicken; stir until cream cheese melts. Spoon 2–3 tablespoons mixture down center of each tortilla; roll up. Place seam side down in greased 9x13-inch baking dish. Sprinkle with cheese and add whipping cream. Bake 30 minutes. Yield: 12 enchiladas

CONFETTI RICE

½ medium onion, chopped
¼ cup each: chopped red, green, and yellow bell peppers
1 (4-ounce) can chopped mushrooms, drained
1 stick margarine
1 cup rice
1 (14.5-ounce) can chicken broth
1 cup water
½ cup slivered almonds, toasted

Preheat oven to 350 degrees. Sauté onion, peppers, and mushrooms in margarine. Combine with remiaining ingredients. Bake in greased 9x13-inch casserole dish for 45 minutes. Yield: 8 servings

SEND GUESTS HOME WITH FAVOR BAGS OF
"NUTS AND BOLTS" MADE BY STIRRING
2 CUPS OF HONEY GRAHAM CEREAL AND
1 CUP OF SALTED PEANUTS INTO
1 (24-OUNCE) PACKAGE OF MELTED WHITE
ALMOND BARK DROPPED BY TEASPOONFULS
ON WAX PAPER. YIELD: 25–30 PIECES

FIESTA CORN

4 (11-ounce) cans Mexican-style, whole-kernel corn
½ cup chopped green onions
¼ cup each: chopped red and green bell pepper
½ cup mayonnaise
1 tablespoon blackened seasoning

Combine ingredients; spoon into pepper halves. Cover and chill 12 hours before serving. Yield: 12 servings

CRANBERRY-NUT COOKIES

1 (17.5-ounce) bag sugar cookie mix
1 stick butter, softened
1 egg
1 (12-ounce) package white chocolate morsels
1 (6-ounce) bag sweetened dried cranberries
1 (6-ounce) can pistachio nuts with cashews and almonds, coarsely chopped

Preheat oven to 375 degrees. Combine cookie mix and butter with mixer. Add egg. Stir in morsels, cranberries, and nuts. Roll into 1-inch balls and place on ungreased cookie sheet. Bake for 8–10 minutes. Cool on a wire rack. Yield: 24 cookies

CHOCOLATE CHIP COOKIES

1¼ cups all-purpose flour
1¼ teaspoons baking soda
½ teaspoon salt
½ cup shortening
¼ cup brown sugar
½ cup sugar
1 tablespoon honey
1 egg, beaten
1 teaspoon each: Grand Marnier and vanilla
1 cup semisweet chocolate chips

Preheat oven to 350 degrees. Combine flour, baking soda, and salt; set aside. Cream shortening and sugars; add honey, egg, Grand Marnier, and vanilla. Gradually blend in dry ingredients. Stir in chocolate chips. Roll into walnut-size balls; press flat on ungreased baking sheets. Bake for 8–10 minutes. Cool 2 minutes; then cool on wire rack. Yield: 24 cookies

KAHLÚA BROWNIES

1 stick butter, melted
2 (1-ounce) squares unsweetened chocolate, melted
¼ cup sugar
½ cup brown sugar
¼ cup kahlúa
1 teaspoon vanilla
2 eggs
½ cup all-purpose flour
¼ teaspoon salt

Preheat oven to 350 degrees. Combine butter and chocolate. Add sugars, kahlúa, and vanilla; add eggs one at a time. Stir in flour and salt. Bake in greased 9x9-inch pan for 20–23 minutes. Cool. Yield: 16 brownies

FROSTING

2 tablespoons butter, softened
1 (1-ounce) square unsweetened chocolate, melted
2 cups confectioners' sugar
1 tablespoon kahlúa
4 tablespoons cream

Beat all ingredients until smooth. Spread over cool brownies.

Flamingo Brunch

A whimsical flamingo bride dressed in a tulle veil and pearls, standing in a bed of flowers and ivy, welcomes guests to a party that promises fun from beginning to end. Guests are seated at different tables featuring flamingos dancing among salmon-colored Gerbera daisies, lime and white mums, and hydrangeas. The bride is definitely the guest of honor in a chair decorated with lace, tulle, ribbons, pearls, and a nosegay of coordinating flowers. The theme and colors of this brunch are memorable and alert everyone to the delightful day ahead. And the light fare of Shrimp Crêpes and salad ensures that every bridesmaid's gown will be a perfect fit!

Great ideas

INVITIATIONS

Invitations to bridesmaids' brunches and luncheons should be sent out three to four weeks prior to the event.

It is a good idea to include Regrets or R.S.V.P., a phone number for questions, and directions to the location on the invitation.

It is nice to include mothers of the bride and groom, grandmothers of the bride and groom, and special aunts and cousins at the bridesmaids' brunch or luncheon.

BRUNCHES ARE TRADITIONALLY HELD AT 10:00 OR 11:00 IN THE MORNING AND USUALLY LAST FOR AN HOUR AND A HALF TO TWO HOURS.

BRIDESMAIDS' GIFTS

Present gifts for bridesmaids in decorated, plastic eggs wrapped in tulle with ribbons and flowers.

Great ideas ——————

SALAD CONTAINERS

Use unexpected containers to serve fruit and vegetable salads.

Fill elegant compotes with greens or fruits with small flowers and place them at each place setting before guests arrive.

Small metal or woven baskets are great for displaying and serving fresh fruit.

Parmesan cheese baskets are delicious and perfect for serving individual green salads. They can be made ahead and stored in tins. To make the baskets, heat a 10-inch nonstick skillet over medium heat. Sprinkle grated Parmesan cheese into the skillet, covering the bottom of the skillet, and heat for about one minute until cheese is lightly browned. Remove the cheese disk from the skillet, place over an aluminum soft drink can, and shape the edges to form a basket.

BRIDESMAIDS' BRUNCHES AND LUNCHEONS
ARE CUSTOMARILY HOSTED BY THE
MAID OR MATRON OF HONOR
AND THE BRIDESMAIDS AND THEIR
FAMILIES, BUT MAY ALSO BE HOSTED
BY SPECIAL FAMILY MEMBERS AND FRIENDS.

Menu

SHRIMP CRÊPES
STRAWBERRY GREEN SALAD
FRESH SEASONAL FRUIT
ICED INDIAN TEA
HEART MERINGUES WITH LEMON
    FILLING AND MELBA SAUCE

SHRIMP CRÊPES

CRÊPE SAUCE

4 tablespoons butter
6 tablespoons all-purpose flour
2 cups canned chicken broth
2 egg yolks
½ cup heavy cream
¾ teaspoon salt
⅛ teaspoon white pepper
¾ teaspoon lemon juice

Melt butter in a 3- or 4-quart saucepan. Remove from heat; stir in flour. Whisk in chicken broth until roux is completely dissolved. Cook over medium heat, stirring constantly, until sauce is smooth and thick. Combine egg yolks with heavy cream. Mix a few tablespoons of simmering sauce into egg mixture. Then, reverse the process, slowly pouring egg mixture into saucepan. Continue to stir. Bring sauce to a boil for 10 seconds. Remove from heat, and add salt, pepper, and lemon juice. Set aside.

THIS CRÊPE RECIPE COULD BE MADE WITH CHICKEN SUBSTITUTED FOR THE SHRIMP. CRÊPES ALSO MAKE WONDERFUL DESSERTS FILLED WITH CREAMY PUDDINGS, SAUCES, AND FRUITS.

CRÊPE FILLING

4 tablespoons butter, divided
3 tablespoons finely chopped scallions
¼ pound (about 1 cup) fresh mushrooms, finely chopped
2 cups frozen, small, peeled, and deveined shrimp
1 tablespoon finely chopped parsley
1 (5-ounce) package Frieda's French Style Crêpes
½ cup heavy cream
4 tablespoons finely grated Swiss cheese

Melt 2 tablespoons butter in frying pan. Add scallions, and sauté about a minute without allowing them to lose color. Add mushrooms. Cook until dry, but not brown. Remove from heat. Add shrimp, parsley, and one cup of Crêpe Filling. Mix. Place 2 tablespoons mixture in lower third of crêpe and roll without tucking the end. Lay side by side in a greased 9x13-inch baking dish. Cover with remaining Crêpe Filling, thinned with ½ cup cream. Sprinkle cheese on top. (May be refrigerated at this point a day before baking.) Preheat oven to 350 degrees. Bake 20 minutes or until sauce bubbles. Yield: 12 crêpes

STRAWBERRY GREEN SALAD

2 cups romaine lettuce
2 cups baby spinach
1 package spring mix salad greens
1 pint fresh strawberries, sliced
1 cup walnuts, sautéed in butter
1 (12-ounce) bottle Brianna's Home Style Blush Wine Vinaigrette Dressing

Toss greens with strawberries and walnuts. Drizzle with dressing just before serving. Yield: 8 servings

Iced Indian Tea

Juice of 4 lemons
5 regular-size tea bags
1 cup boiling water
1 tablespoon almond flavoring
1 tablespoon vanilla extract
4 cups water
1½ cups sugar
1 quart ginger ale

Combine lemon juice, tea bags, and boiling water. Cover and let stand for 20 minutes. Add next 4 ingredients. Chill. Add ginger ale just before serving. Yield: 1 gallon

Heart Meringues with Lemon Filling and Melba Sauce

MERINGUE SHELL HEARTS

3 large egg whites, at room temperature
½ teaspoon vanilla
¼ teaspoon cream of tartar
1 cup sugar

Let egg whites stand at room temperature in a large mixing bowl for about 30 minutes. Preheat oven to 300 degrees. Cover a baking sheet with nonstick foil. Draw eight (3-inch) hearts by tracing a cookie cutter for individual shells. Add vanilla and cream of tartar to egg whites. Beat with mixer on medium speed until soft peaks form (tips curl). Add sugar, one tablespoon at a time, beating on high speed, until stiff peaks form (tips stand straight) and sugar is almost dissolved. Spread or pipe meringue over hearts on foil, building up the edges to shape into shells. Bake for 30 minutes. Turn oven off; let dry in oven with door closed for at least one hour (do not open door). Peel meringues off foil. Store in an airtight container. Yield: 8 shells

LEMON FILLING

1 (14-ounce) can sweetened condensed milk
2 egg yolks
⅓ cup lemon juice

Combine ingredients with mixer; chill. Yield: 2 cups

MELBA SAUCE

1 (12-ounce) package frozen, unsweetened raspberries, thawed
2 tablespoons sugar
1 tablespoon orange juice

Heat thawed raspberries with their juice in a saucepan; press purée through a fine mesh sieve into a bowl. Discard seeds. Stir sugar and orange juice into purée. Yield: 1½ cups

TO ASSEMBLE

1 (6-ounce) package fresh raspberries
For garnish: whipped topping and fresh mint

Drizzle or drop dots of Melba Sauce from a squeeze bottle onto each plate. Place meringue on plate. Spoon about 2 tablespoons Lemon Filling into heart meringue. Arrange berries hulled end down over filling. Garnish with whipped topping and fresh mint. Yield: 8 servings

CREATE HEARTS ON THE
SERVING PLATE BY DROPPING DOTS
OF MELBA SAUCE ONTO THE PLATE
FROM A SQUEEZE BOTTLE
AND SHAPING THEM INTO HEARTS
WITH A TOOTHPICK.

Swan Luncheon

Swans mate for life, thus creating a very appropriate and elegant motif for this bridesmaids' luncheon. Handsome glass swan containers can be found at antiques stores, flea markets, and gift shops. When filled with fresh flowers, they become the center of attention on every table. The tiny gold swans filled with mini bouquets and holding name cards for the bride and her bridesmaids began as white plastic "ugly ducklings" from a craft store. Begin the luncheon with Asparagus Soup and Spicy Cheese Hearts followed by a chicken entrée over rice, green beans, and strawberry salads shaped like hearts. The graceful Cream Puff Swans swimming in chocolate sauce complete the theme.

Great ideas

FRONT DOOR

Greet guests with a wreath of lemon leaves and baby's breath tied in satin bows with golden hearts.

MENUS

Make a menu card for each plate on the computer in a nice font and coordinating color. Punch a hole at the top, and add a ribbon or tassel.

PLACE CARD HOLDERS

The tiny gold swans filled with mini bouquets and holding name cards began as white plastic "ugly ducklings" from a craft store.

BRIDESMAIDS' GIFT

Give a personal book made with pictures and memories or special recipes to each bridesmaid and mothers and grandmothers. These can be made at blurb.com. or shutterfly.com.

Menu

ASPARAGUS SOUP
SPICY CHEESE HEARTS
CELEBRATION CHICKEN OVER RICE
STRAWBERRY SALAD HEARTS
GREAT GREEN BEANS
ROLLS AND HONEY-ALMOND
   BUTTER
CREAM PUFF SWANS IN CHOCOLATE
   SAUCE

ASPARAGUS SOUP

2 cups milk
4 tablespoons butter
4 tablespoon all-purpose flour
1 teaspoon salt
2 (15-ounce) cans asparagus pieces
1 quart chicken broth
½ teaspoon black pepper
½ teaspoon white pepper
2 tablespoons cornstarch
½ cup cold water
For garnish: sour cream and fresh parsley

Combine milk, butter, flour, and salt in a large saucepan and heat, stirring continually, to make a cream sauce. Add asparagus, broth, and peppers slowly to cream sauce. Combine cornstarch with cold water and mix well. Add to soup and simmer for 15 minutes. Do not boil. Serve hot. Garnish with sour cream and fresh parsley. Yield: 10–12 servings

TO THICKEN SAUCES, USE
CORNSTARCH ADDED TO COLD WATER,
OR FLOUR ADDED TO HOT WATER.

SPICY CHEESE HEARTS

8 ounces sharp Cheddar cheese, grated
½ cup butter, softened
½ teaspoon salt
½ teaspoon cayenne pepper, plus more for sprinkling
1½ cups all-purpose flour

Preheat oven to 350 degrees. Cream cheese and butter, then add seasonings. Add flour to form stiff dough. Roll out ¼ inch thick on a floured surface. Cut out wafers with a small heart-shaped cookie cutter or press through a cookie press using a heart disk. Place on a greased cookie sheet. Sprinkle lightly with cayenne pepper. Bake about 25 minutes or until lightly browned. Yield: 5 dozen

STRAWBERRY SALAD HEARTS

1 (21-ounce) can strawberry pie filling
½ cup sugar
1 (3-ounce) package strawberry gelatin
1 (8-ounce) can crushed pineapple, drained
½ cup chopped pecans
For garnish: leaf lettuce, fresh berries, fresh mint, and
    whipped topping

Combine pie filling and sugar; bring to a boil in a sauce-pan or in the microwave. Add pineapple and nuts. Pour mixture into 12 heart-shaped molds that have been sprayed with nonstick cooking spray. Refrigerate until firm. When ready to serve, dip bottom of mold in warm water, and turn salad onto a piece of leaf lettuce. Garnish with whipped topping and a fanned strawberry or berries. May also be made with cherry pie filling and cherry gelatin. Yield: 12 servings

GREAT GREEN BEANS

6 (14.5-ounce) cans whole green beans
½ stick butter
½ cup light brown sugar, packed
½ cup crumbled bacon

Preheat oven to 325 degrees. Drain green beans, and pour into a 9x13-inch baking dish. Set aside. Melt butter, and stir in brown sugar. Pour butter and sugar mixture over green beans. Sprinkle with crumbled bacon. Cover with foil and bake for 30 minutes. Yield: 10–12 servings

CELEBRATION CHICKEN

1 cup sliced almonds, toasted, divided
1 (2.25-ounce) jar sliced dried beef
6 boneless, skinless chicken breasts
White pepper, paprika, onion salt, and celery salt to taste
12 strips bacon
2 (10.75-ounce) cans cream of mushroom soup
1 cup sour cream
1 (8-ounce) package cream cheese, softened
1 (7.3-ounce) jar sliced mushrooms, drained
Rice, cooked
For garnish: sprigs of parsley

Toast almonds on a cookie sheet in a 350-degree oven for 10 minutes and set aside. Preheat oven to 275 degrees. Grease a 9x13-inch pan with nonstick cooking spray. Spread sliced dried beef on bottom of pan in a single layer. Cut each chicken breast into 2 small strips. Sprinkle each very lightly with pepper, paprika, onion salt, and celery salt. Fold each strip into a roll with spices on inside; wrap a piece of bacon on the outside, and secure with a toothpick. Place each chicken roll on top of a piece of dried beef. Combine soup, sour cream, and cream cheese. Fold in mushrooms and ½ cup almonds. Pour over chicken breasts. Cover with foil, and bake 2½ hours. Remove foil, and lightly brown for 30 minutes. Serve over rice. Sprinkle with remaining almonds and garnish with a few sprigs parsley. Yield: 12 servings

WHEN SEATING A BRIDESMAIDS' LUNCHEON, PLACE THE BRIDE AT THE HEAD OF THE TABLE WITH HER MAID OR MATRON OF HONOR ON HER RIGHT.

Rolls

1 cup warm water
1 tablespoon rapid rise yeast
1 tablespoon sugar
3 cups bread flour
1 teaspoon salt
2 tablespoons olive oil

Heat water in microwave 30 seconds. Mix in yeast and sugar until foamy; set aside. Place flour and salt into food processor. Pour in olive oil and pulse for 30 seconds. Add yeast mixture and process 20–30 seconds. Place dough in bowl and let rise 30 minutes to one hour. For cloverleaf rolls, roll dough into small balls. Place 3 small balls into each cup of a greased muffin tin. Let rise 15 minutes. Bake at 400 degrees for 10–12 minutes. Yield: 2 dozen rolls

HONEY-ALMOND BUTTER

1 cup butter, softened
2 ounces honey
½ teaspoon almond extract

Blend butter, honey, and almond extract together in mixer. Do not overmix.

SPREAD SOFTENED BUTTER INTO
HEART-SHAPED MOLDS AND FREEZE.

Cream Puff Swans

1 cup water
4 tablespoons butter, cubed
1 cup all-purpose flour
4 eggs
1 egg for glazing
1 teaspoon water
Filling: ice cream or instant vanilla mousse pudding,
    prepared according to package directions
Chocolate sauce
Confectioners' sugar, for dusting

For cream puffs, in a saucepan, bring water and butter to a boil. Add flour all at once, stirring until a smooth ball forms. Remove from the heat; let stand for 5 minutes. Add 4 eggs, one at a time, beating well after each addition. Continue beating until mixture is smooth. For swan bodies drop by rounded tablespoonfuls 3 inches apart on greased baking sheet lined with parchment. For necks, on a separate parchment-lined baking sheet, pipe S-shaped necks using a #11 small round tip and pastry bag. Mix remaining egg and water, and brush lightly over bodies and necks. Bake bodies at 400 degrees for 30-35 minutes or until golden brown and necks about 10 minutes. Remove to wire racks. Immediately split puffs and remove tops; discard soft dough from inside. Set puffs and tops aside to cool.

To assemble: Spoon chocolate sauce onto plate. Place bottom half of body in chocolate sauce and cut top of puff in half making 2 wings. Fill swan body with ice cream or mousse. Put wings on sides, and place neck into filling. Dust plate with confectioners' sugar, and garnish with a pansy or Johnny-Jump-Up. Yield: 12 servings

FOR A SPECIAL GARNISH, ADD SUGARED,
PESTISIDE-FREE FLOWERS TO DESSERT
PLATES. BRUSH PETALS WITH AN EGG WHITE
BEATEN WITH A TEASPOON OF WATER
AND SPRINKLE WITH SUGAR.

Favorite Ladies' Luncheon

Girls love pink! Line the table for the bride and her favorite ladies with French altar candlesticks and simple rustic urns of hydrangeas and several shades of pink roses. Add sheer, pink organza napkins tied into large floppy bows with vintage pins in the center of the knots and floral pink china on gold chargers. The Almond Chicken in a heart puff pastry is delicious, and the Cold Melon Soup echoes the color scheme. Desserts are miniature, tiered wedding cakes with silver charms on ribbons underneath. The charms tell who will be the next to get married, who will go on the next trip, who will go to grad school, and who will have the first baby. Send each bridesmaid's charm and vintage pin home in a lacy heart box made by gluing a heart-shaped doily to the top and the bottom of a small white jewelry box and enhance the top with ribbons and silk flowers. Give each bridesmaid, mother of the bride, mother of the groom, and the flower girl a large white shopping bag, decorated with her name in gold letters, to be taken to the wedding dressing room to store belongings while dressing for the wedding.

Great ideas

A SPECIAL FAVOR

As a special favor, place a photograph of the bride with each guest in a small frame as a place card.

PERSONALIZE

Give the bridesmaids, mother of the bride, mother of the groom, and the flower girl large white shopping bags, decorated with their name in gold letters, to be taken to the wedding dressing room to store belongings while dressing for the wedding.

BRIDESMAIDS' GIFTS

Send each bridesmaid's charm and vintage pin home in a lacy heart box made by gluing a heart-shaped doily to the top and the bottom of a small white jewelry box. Enhance the top with ribbons and silk flowers.

COLD MELON SOUP
PEAR SALAD WITH CANDIED WALNUTS
ALMOND CHICKEN IN PUFF PASTRY
BAKED ASPARAGUS
MINI WEDDING CAKES WITH CHARMS

COLD MELON SOUP

1 quart vanilla ice cream, melted
1 small watermelon, puréed
1 teaspoon vanilla
For garnish: mint sprigs

Let ice cream melt in a bowl in the refrigerator. Cut watermelon and remove rind, white pieces, and seeds. Purée watermelon chunks in food processor. Combine purée, ice cream, and vanilla. Keep in the refrigerator. Garnish with mint sprigs. Yield: 12–16 servings

PEAR SALAD WITH CANDIED WALNUTS

CANDIED WALNUTS

9 tablespoons sugar, divided
3 tablespoons orange juice
2 cups walnut halves
1 teaspoon cinnamon

Preheat oven to 350 degrees. Line cookie sheet with foil and spray with nonstick cooking spray. In a skillet over medium heat, combine 6 tablespoons sugar with orange juice, and bring to a simmer. Add walnuts, and heat until sugar mixture is absorbed and nuts begin to caramelize, 2–3 minutes, stirring constantly. Cool slightly, and toss nuts in a mixture of 3 tablespoons sugar and cinnamon. Bake on prepared cookie sheet for about 3 minutes.

PEAR SALAD

1 (8-ounce) package cream cheese, softened
4 ounces blue cheese, crumbled
Bibb lettuce
4 fresh pears, cored and cut into 4 slices each
1 orange, sliced
2 kiwis, peeled and sliced
8 whole strawberries with leaves attached
Balsamic vinaigrette

Combine cream cheese and blue cheese and set aside.

To assemble salad, place a leaf of lettuce on plate. Add two pear slices, one orange slice, one kiwi slice, and one whole strawberry. Drizzle with vinaigrette. Add a spoonful of cream cheese mixture and sprinkle with Candied Walnuts. Yield: 8 servings

ALMOND CHICKEN IN PUFF PASTRY

PUFF PASTRY

1 pound frozen puff pastry, thawed (or packaged frozen puff pastry shells)

Preheat oven to 425 degrees. For heart-shaped pastry, roll out pastry in 2 squares on a lightly floured surface. Cut 4 large hearts from each square with a heart-shaped cookie cutter. With a smaller heart cutter, cut a small heart halfway through the dough in the center of each large heart for a removable heart in order to fill pastries. Bake on a cookie sheet for 10 minutes. Yield: 8 pastries

CHICKEN FILLING

1 cup slivered almonds, divided
1 cup sliced fresh mushrooms
½ cup plus 3 tablespoons butter, divided
½ cup all-purpose flour
1 cup half-and-half
1 cup chicken broth
1 cup milk
3 cups cooked and diced chicken breasts
1 teaspoon salt
½ cup sherry

Toast almonds on a cookie sheet at 350 degrees for 10 minutes; set aside. Sauté mushrooms in 3 tablespoons butter until tender; set aside. In a saucepan over medium heat, melt remaining ½ cup butter; add flour and stir for about 1 minute, until smooth. Gradually add half-and-half, broth, and milk, stirring constantly until combined and thickened. Fold in mushrooms, chicken, salt, sherry, and ¾ cup almonds.

To serve, remove small heart from pastry shell and fill with Chicken Filling. Garnish with remaining almonds, and replace top. Yield: 8 servings

Baked Asparagus

1 pound fresh small asparagus, trimmed
Olive oil
Lemon pepper
Sesame seeds

Preheat oven to 450 degrees. Wash asparagus. Break off bottoms at natural break point. Place tops on a cookie sheet. Drizzle with olive oil and sprinkle with lemon pepper and sesame seeds. Bake until slightly brown, 7–10 minutes. They will still be a little bit crisp. Yield: 8 servings

Mini Wedding Cakes with Charms

CAKE

1 (18.25-ounce) super moist white cake mix
1 teaspoon clear vanilla extract
1 teaspoon almond extract (optional)
1 teaspoon butter flavoring

For cake, follow package directions, using egg whites only, then add flavorings. Bake in greased 9x13-inch cake pan according to package directions. (Make several recipes as needed.) It is important that the cakes bake evenly. After cake is cooled, turn out on a cake board. Cover with plastic wrap and foil and freeze. When frozen, cut a 3-inch circle with cookie cutter for each bridesmaid's cake. Cut one 4-inch base circle, one 3-inch circle, and one 1½-inch circle for the bride's three-tiered cake. Place each cake on wax paper, and place on small turntable to ice. Prepare Buttercream Icing. On each cake, pre-ice an almost transparent layer

of icing using a spatula to eliminate crumbs. Then, ice with a thicker second layer; make smooth using a bit of warm water on the spatula, if necessary. Allow each layer to set a few minutes, then "iron" top of cake with the smooth side of a paper towel directly on the cake, using a sweeping motion with a spatula. Place a charm attached to a ribbon on the bottom of each bridesmaids' dessert plate. Place cake over charm with spatula and pipe borders and flowers on each bridesmaid cake and on each layer of the bride's cake.

BUTTERCREAM ICING

1 cup shortening
1 teaspoon clear vanilla
1 teaspoon almond extract
1 teaspoon butter flavoring
1 (1-pound) box confectioners' sugar
1 pinch salt
½–1 cup whole milk

In a large mixing bowl, using mixer, blend shortening and flavorings. Add confectioners' sugar slowly. Add salt. The mixture will become very stiff. When blended completely, add ½ cup milk. Test for icing consistency. Add milk, one tablespoon at a time, until the icing is smooth and silky. The icing should be very easy to spread. For flowers and leaves, which are piped directly onto the cakes, add more confectioners' sugar to the Buttercream Icing to stiffen texture. For roses and more intricate flowers, add small amounts of cornstarch to the icing and make flowers separately on a rose nail. Let dry on wax paper. These can be made in advance and stored in a cookie tin for several days.

SILVER CHARMS ARE AVAILABLE FROM
ExclusivelyWeddings.com.

Tying the Knot

Neckties and *The Wall Street Journal*-wrapped boxes with ticker tape establish the theme for this luncheon for the groom and his groomsmen, while meat, vegetables, cornbread, and sweet tea with cheesecake and apple pie are on the menu for the big day. Neckties from generous friends, relatives, and thrift stores for one dollar each were used to create these starburst placemats and small necktie napkin rings. Twelve large tie ends are glued around the edge of a circle of fabric with fabric glue for each placemat; the thin end of the ties are tied with Windsor knots to form small necktie napkin rings. Napkins are initialed men's handkerchiefs for each groomsman to keep. Containers for pots of ivy are square boxes wrapped in *The Wall Street Journal* with strips of white paper rolled around a pencil to curl like ticker tapes. The groomsmen's gifts are wrapped in *The Wall Street Journal* and tied with their bow ties for the wedding. So after their very business lunch, the guys will all be ready for the activities and festivities of the day.

Great ideas

Wrap groomsmen's gifts in small, square boxes covered with The Wall Street Journal *and tied with the bow tie that is to be worn at the wedding.*

For table arrangements, place small pots of ivy into square boxes wrapped in The Wall Street Journal, *accented with ticker tapes made of curled strips of white paper.*

RESPONSIBILITIES OF THE GROOMSMEN AND THE BEST MAN

Groomsmen and the best man should help the groom with tasks to prepare for the wedding and give friendship and support.

They should be fitted and rent attire for the wedding.

They should help with a bachelor's party.

They should attend as many parties prior to the wedding as possible.

They should attend the groomsmen's brunch or luncheon.

They should attend the rehearsal and rehearsal dinner.

They should arrive for the wedding one hour early.

They should usher guests to their seats for the ceremony. The bride's family is seated to the left and the groom's family is seated to the right.

They should be in a group to catch the bride's garter, unless they are married.

They should decorate the going-away car.

They should remain at the reception until the bride and groom leave for the honeymoon.

RESPONSIBILITIES OF THE BEST MAN AT THE WEDDING

During the wedding, the best man stands beside the groom as he waits for his bride to come down the aisle.

If there is no ring bearer, he has the bride's wedding ring for the exchanging of rings in the ceremony.

Menu

ROAST WITH CARROTS AND POTATOES
SKILLET CABBAGE
STUFFED SQUASH
D.G.'S CORNBREAD
SWEET TEA
CHEESECAKE PIE
SOUR CREAM APPLE PIE

ROAST WITH CARROTS AND POTATOES

1 (3½-pound) boneless pot roast
Salt and pepper to taste
All-purpose flour
¼ cup oil
1 (1.25-ounce) package Lipton Onion Soup mix
½ cup water
1 (1-pound) package peeled mini carrots
2 pounds new red potatoes

Wash roast, trim excess fat, and sprinkle with salt and pepper. Coat sides with flour. Heat oil in Dutch oven and brown roast on both sides. Add soup mix and water, and stir. Cover and lower heat to simmer. Simmer 3 hours, turning roast every 15 minutes. Add carrots and potatoes after 2½ hours. Cool roast, slice, and serve with gravy. Yield: 8 servings

SKILLET CABBAGE

3 slices bacon
½ cup water
6 cups shredded cabbage
½ teaspoon sugar
Salt and pepper to taste

Fry bacon in heavy skillet. Remove bacon and add water. Add cabbage, sugar, salt, and pepper. Cover and cook over medium heat for 15–20 minutes. Serve with crumbled bacon. Yield: 8 servings

STUFFED SQUASH

4 yellow squash
3 tablespoons chopped bell pepper
¼ cup chopped onion
¼ cup butter, divided
½ cup shredded Cheddar cheese
⅓ cup sour cream
¼ cup real bacon bits
½ cup fine bread crumbs

Preheat oven to 350 degrees. Boil squash in water to cover until tender, but firm. Slice lengthwise and remove pulp; set aside. Sauté pepper and onion in 2 tablespoons butter. Combine pulp, pepper, onion, cheese, sour cream, and bacon bits; stuff squash halves. Sprinkle with crumbs and dot with remaining butter. Bake for 10–15 minutes. Yield: 8 servings

D.G.'S CORNBREAD

2 cups self-rising cornmeal
1 cup self-rising flour
1 cup sugar
⅛ teaspoon baking soda
1 egg, beaten
1 cup buttermilk
⅓ cup vegetable oil

Preheat oven to 425 degrees. Combine cornmeal, flour, sugar, and soda. Add egg and buttermilk. Heat oil in a 10-inch iron skillet in the oven. Remove skillet and pour oil into mixture. Pour batter into skillet and bake for 20–25 minutes. Yield: 8 servings

SWEET TEA

8 cups water
2 family-size tea bags
2 cups sugar
To garnish: lemon slices and mint

Bring water to a rolling boil. Remove from heat; add tea bags. Steep, covered, for 6–24 hours. Warm tea; but do not boil. Stir in sugar until dissolved. Add additional cold water to make a gallon. Serve over ice with lemon slices and mint. Yield: 1 gallon

CHEESECAKE PIE

½ cup toasted and chopped pecans
1 (9-inch) deep-dish pie crust
2 (8-ounce) packages cream cheese, softened
½ cup sugar
⅓ cup sour cream
1 teaspoon each: vanilla and almond extract
1 teaspoon self-rising flour
2 eggs, beaten
1 (21-ounce) can blueberry pie filling
For garnish: whipped topping, mint, and blueberries

Preheat oven to 350 degrees. Press pecans into bottom of pie crust. Prick bottom and sides of crust. Bake 5 minutes and cool.

Combine cream cheese, sugar, sour cream, vanilla, and almond extract with mixer on low. Add flour and eggs. Pour into pie crust. Bake 40–45 minutes. Cool pie, then chill. To serve, top with pie filling and whipped topping. Garnish with mint and berries. Yield: 8 servings

MAMA JAN'S "PERFECTLY EASY" PIE CRUST

In a small bowl, sift just over 1 cup all-purpose flour and ½ teaspoon salt. Make a hole in the center of the mixture. Pour ¼ cup plus 2 tablespoons vegetable oil and 3 tablespoons milk into the hole. Incorporate flour until well blended. Place crust into pie pan and flatten, pushing toward the sides and up the edges until pan is covered. Bake in preheated, 400-degree oven for 10–12 minutes.

SOUR CREAM APPLE PIE

2 tablespoons all-purpose flour
¾ cup sugar
⅛ teaspoon salt
1 egg, unbeaten
1 cup sour cream
1 teaspoon vanilla
¼ teaspoon nutmeg
1 (21-ounce) can apple pie filling
1 (9-inch) pie crust, unbaked

Preheat oven to 400 degrees. Sift flour, sugar, and salt together. Add egg, sour cream, vanilla, and nutmeg. Beat with a wooden spoon until smooth. Stir in pie filling. Pour into crust and bake for 10 minutes. Reduce heat to 350 degrees and bake for 30 minutes. Remove from oven and add Spicy Topping; return to oven and bake at 400 degrees for 10 minutes. Yield: 6 servings

SPICY TOPPING

⅓ cup sugar
⅓ cup all-purpose flour
1 teaspoon cinnamon
¼ cup butter, softened

Mix ingredients together with a fork and spread over partially cooked pie.

Rehearsal Dinner

The wedding rehearsal is over and the proxy bride has played her part. This very special dinner, following the rehearsal, is a memory that the bride and groom will cherish for the rest of their lives. Everyone they love and everyone who has played an important part in their lives and shaped them into the people that they have become are in this very room for one enchanted evening, celebrating their love, joy, commitment, and new life together. Tables are dressed for the occasion in the finest lace, linens, china, crystal, and silver. Elegant arrangements of white hydrangeas, roses, lilies, and tulips are layered on gold-edged ruffle cake plates in the center of each round table with small cupid vases holding a few stems above each place setting. Chairs wear cream silk seat covers with wide bows and long streamers. The seats of honor are draped with white dendrobian orchid garlands and the bride's chair has a small nosegay tied to the side with a wide, satin ribbon. As guests arrive, they are greeted with Crawfish Beignets and sips of Roasted Garlic Soup in tiny glasses and a fromage platter followed by a salad. Dinner is Peppercorn Tenderloin in Puff Pastry, Potato Casserole, and Haricot Verts with Pecan Roulade for a sweet ending—and beginning.

WEDDING PARTIES

Menu

ROASTED GARLIC SOUP

CRAWFISH BEIGNETS WITH BRANDIED TOMATO SAUCE

FROMAGE PLATTER

GREENS WITH FIGS AND SHERRY VINAIGRETTE

PEPPERCORN TENDERLOIN IN PUFF PASTRY

POTATO CASSEROLE

HARICOT VERTS

PECAN ROULADE WITH PRALINE MOUSSE

ROASTED GARLIC SOUP

2 tablespoons butter
2 tablespoons olive oil
2 cups chopped onions
1 cup peeled garlic cloves
1 teaspoon fresh thyme
3 cups chicken broth
1 cup stale French bread, torn into pieces
½ cup heavy cream
For garnish: butter and fresh chopped parsley

Heat butter and oil in saucepan with heavy bottom over low to medium heat. Add onions and garlic and cook for 30–40 minutes until golden brown. Add thyme and broth and bring to a boil. Stir in bread and simmer 10 minutes. Remove from heat and cool. Purée soup in blender; add cream. Serve in small glasses. Yield: 50 servings

PRETTY PRESENTATIONS—RIM SOUP GLASSES WITH BUTTER AND DIP IN CHOPPED PARSLEY. SPRINKLE FRESH HERBS AND FINELY DICED VEGETABLES ON PLATES AS COLORFUL CONFETTI.

CRAWFISH BEIGNETS WITH BRANDIED TOMATO SAUCE

2 cups all-purpose flour
2 teaspoons baking powder
1½ cups soda water
½ pound crawfish tails, chopped
1 red bell pepper, chopped
1 bunch scallions, chopped
1 clove garlic, minced
2 teaspoons lemon zest
2 teaspoons salt
2 teaspoons hot sauce
Vegetable oil

Sift flour and baking powder; whisk in soda water until blended. Stir in crawfish, bell pepper, scallions, garlic, and zest. Season with salt and hot sauce. Heat one inch of oil in skillet over medium heat. Drop batter by spoonfuls into oil; turn until golden brown. Drain on paper towels and serve with Brandied Tomato Sauce. Yield: 24 beignets

BRANDIED TOMATO SAUCE

1 cup mayonnaise
2 teaspoons lemon juice
2 tablespoons cream
⅓ cup ketchup
1 tablespoon brandy
1 tablespoon chopped basil

Mix all ingredients.

Greens with Figs and Sherry Vinaigrette

3–4 cups mixed greens
6 dried mission figs, reconstituted in warm water
⅓ cup toasted, chopped walnuts
¼ cup blue cheese, crumbled
1 shallot, chopped

Toss greens, figs, walnuts, and blue cheese in bowl. Plate and drizzle with Sherry Vinaigrette. Yield: 4 servings

Sherry Vinaigrette

2 tablespoons sherry vinegar
1 tablespoon honey
2 teaspoons rinsed and chopped capers
1 teaspoon Dijon mustard
½ cup olive oil
Salt and pepper to taste

Whisk all ingredients together and drizzle over salad. Yield: ¾ cup

Peppercorn Tenderloin in Puff Pastry

1 (1½- to 2-pound) peppercorn tenderloin
1 (17.3-ounce) package puff pastry, 2 sheets
1 egg white

Preheat oven to 350 degrees. Place tenderloin on foil-lined pan and bake 45 minutes or until temperature reaches 170 degrees on a meat thermometer. Remove from oven and cool completely. Trim ends and wrap in one sheet of puff pastry, sealing edges on bottom with egg white. Cut flowers and leaves from other sheet of pastry and secure on top with egg white. Brush top with egg white and bake for 10–15 minutes. Yield: 6–8 servings

Potato Casserole

5 pounds potatoes, peeled, boiled, and drained
½ onion, chopped
2 tablespoons plus ½ cup butter, divided
1 (8-ounce) package cream cheese, softened
1 (8-ounce) carton sour cream
½ cup chopped chives
½ teaspoon salt
½ teaspoon black pepper
½ pint whipping cream, whipped
6 ounces shredded Cheddar cheese
½ cup real bacon bits

Preheat oven to 350 degrees. Whip potatoes; set aside. Sauté onion in 2 tablespoons butter; set aside. Combine remaining ½ cup melted butter, cream cheese, sour cream, chives, salt, pepper, and onion with mixer. Fold in potatoes. Spread into a greased 9x13-inch casserole dish. Top with whipped cream. Sprinkle with cheese and bacon bits. Bake for 20 minutes. Yield: 10–12 servings

The rehearsal Dinner should be given by the groom's parents.

Haricot Verts

1 pound fresh haricot vert beans
3 tablespoons butter
Juice of 1 lemon
½ cup sliced almonds, toasted

In a medium-size pan, bring one inch of salted water to a boil. Place beans in pan or in steamer insert. Steam for 4 minutes, remove from heat, and plunge into ice water for 3–4 minutes. For sauce, melt butter and add lemon juice and toasted almonds. Warm beans in 350-degree oven 5 minutes and drizzle with sauce. Yield: 4 servings

Pecan Roulade with Praline Mousse

1 cup lightly toasted and finely chopped pecans
½ teaspoon baking powder
7 eggs, separated
½ cup sugar, divided

Line a 9x13-inch baking sheet with parchment paper and spray with nonstick cooking spray. Preheat oven to 375 degrees. Toss nuts with the baking powder and set aside. Whip egg yolks with ¼ cup sugar with mixer on high until thick and pale. Stir in nuts. With a clean beater and a clean bowl, whip egg whites on high until soft peaks begin to form and gradually add remaining sugar. Fold whites into the yolk mixture a half at a time. Do not overmix! Spread batter into the prepared pan. Bake 10–12 minutes, until golden brown. Remove from the oven and cover with a damp towel; cool completely. When cool, invert cake onto the damp towel and roll cake up in the towel, jellyroll fashion. Set aside. Prepare Praline Syrup and Praline Mousse.

To assemble, unroll cake and remove parchment. Spread cake with Praline Mousse, and starting with the short edge, gently roll cake up jellyroll fashion. Place the cake back onto the pan and refrigerate for at least 1 hour. To serve, sprinkle cake with confectioners' sugar, cut slices about one inch thick, and drizzle with reserved Praline Syrup. Yield: 8–10 servings

Praline Syrup

1 cup sugar
½ cup water
1 cup cream
1 teaspoon vanilla

Heat sugar and water in a small pan. Heat cream in a separate pan. Bring the sugar mixture to a boil and then hold at a simmer until liquid turns dark golden color. Remove from heat and immediately whisk in the cream and vanilla. Continue stirring as the mixture bubbles until completely smooth. Refrigerate. Yield: 1½ cups

Praline Mousse

½ (8-ounce) package cream cheese, softened
1 cup Praline Syrup
1 teaspoon vanilla
½ teaspoon unflavored gelatin
1 tablespoon warm water
1½ tablespoons dark rum
1 cup cream, whipped to firm peaks

Beat cream cheese in mixer until smooth. Slowly add the Praline Syrup, scraping bowl frequently. Place gelatin in a small bowl with warm water. Add rum to the gelatin and stir to dissolve. Fold gelatin mixture into Praline Syrup mixture; fold in whipped cream.

Hydrangea Brunch

This party is decorated entirely with blue and white. Blue hydrangeas, irises, and delphiniums are combined with white roses and Queen Ann's Lace in blue and white vases and cachepots everywhere, from the food tables to the seating tables spread throughout the garden. Brunch Casserole, Lemon Pepper Green Beans, seasonal fruits, and various rolls and buns are served on everyone's favorite blue willow plates with white linen napkins. Dessert is a light angel food cake with strawberries and whipped cream. This early morning brunch allows friends and family to meet and visit over a leisurely meal before the wedding.

FLOWER POWER

The best time to cut flowers is either early in the morning or after the sun has gone down in the afternoon. Choose sturdy blossoms rather than fresh new growth.

To allow maximum water absorption, cut soft stems at an angle and crush wooded stems. Place freshly cut stems in a clean container of tepid water. Keep in a cool place, away from sunshine and drafts for at least two hours before arranging. Add or replace water daily.

When using floral foam, wet thoroughly and always place the block with the holes on top or bottom to retain water.

To encourage blooms, especially roses and lilies, place in warm water.

Wrap tulips in wet newspaper and place in cool water until use.

Gardenias and camellias absorb water through their petals after being cut, so the entire flower should be wrapped in wet paper towels until used.

Wilted hydrangeas may be revived by placing the flower mops in room temperature water for a few hours.

To dry hydrangeas, collect the flowers near the end of their growing season when the blooms appear paper-like and before they are faded. These blooms, known as immortelles, can be hung in bunches by their stems in a warm, dark place or placed upright in a vase with a few inches of water in a well ventilated place until the water evaporates.

KEEP IT FRESH

A blue-and-white color scheme is always fresh. Decorate seating tables with topiaries of different flowers in the same color family, placed in similar reproduction containers that are reasonable and readily available. These arrangements add height to the tables and are a perfect combination with white cloths and blue willow plates.

Menu

BRUNCH CASSEROLE
LEMON PEPPER GREEN BEANS
SEASONAL FRUIT
CORN SOUFFLÉS
BISCUITS WITH JAM
CINNAMON ROLLS
STICKY BUNS
SHARI'S STRAWBERRY SHORTCAKE
APPLE JUICE COOLER

BRUNCH CASSEROLE

1 (8-ounce) can crescent rolls
1 pound ground pork sausage, fried and drained
1 (32-ounce) package frozen hash brown potatoes with
    onions and peppers, prepared
1 cup shredded Cheddar cheese
4 eggs
½ cup milk
½ teaspoon each: salt, nutmeg, black and white pepper

Preheat oven to 375 degrees. Unroll crescent rolls; press on bottom and partially up sides of 9x13-inch baking dish. Seal perforations. Bake 5 minutes. Sprinkle sausage over crust, then hash browns, then cheese. Cover; chill up to 24 hours. Whisk eggs, milk, salt, nutmeg, and peppers; pour over cheese. Bake 30–35 minutes at 350 degrees. Yield: 8-10 servings

LEMON PEPPER GREEN BEANS

6 (14.5-ounce) cans green beans, drained
½ stick butter
¼ cup sliced almonds
2 teaspoons lemon pepper
For garnish: cherry tomatoes, halved

Preheat oven to 325 degrees. Place green beans in a 9x13-inch baking dish. Sauté almonds in butter and lemon pepper. Sprinkle over beans. Cover; bake 30 minutes. Garnish with tomatos. Yield: 8–10 servings

CORN SOUFFLÉS

1 (8.5-ounce) package cornbread mix
1 (11-ounce) can white shoepeg corn, drained
1 (14.5-ounce) can cream corn
1 cup sour cream
½ stick butter, melted

Preheat oven to 350 degrees. Combine all ingredients and pour into greased muffin tins. Bake for 15–20 minutes. Yield: 12 servings

BISCUITS WITH JAM

1 cup-self rising flour
1½ cups buttermilk
½ cup vegetable shortening

Preheat oven to 400 degrees. Combine flour, buttermilk, and shortening. Dough will be sticky. Knead dough; roll out on floured surface and cut out with a 2-inch cutter. Place in a greased iron skillet and dot tops with shortening. Bake for 15–20 minutes. Yield: 18 biscuits

STRAWBERRY JAM

2 quarts strawberries
1 (1.75-ounce) box Sure-Jell fruit pectin
7 cups sugar

Wash and stem berries. Crush, one layer at a time, to let juice flow freely. Measure 4½ cups berries into saucepan; mix in Sure-Jell. Place over high heat and stir until mixture reaches a hard boil. Add sugar all at once; mix well. Bring to a full rolling boil for one minute, stirring constantly. Remove from heat; skim off foam with metal spoon. Stir and skim for 5 minutes to cool slightly and prevent floating fruit. Quickly ladle into sterilized jars and seal at once. Yield: 8½ pints

WHEN EATING ROLLS, BISCUITS,
OR BREAD, BREAK OFF AND SPREAD
BUTTER ON ONE BITE AT A TIME.

CINNAMON ROLLS

2 packages yeast
1 pint warm water
2 eggs, well beaten
2 sticks butter, melted
1 cup sugar, divided
6 cups all-purpose flour
1 teaspoon salt
½ stick butter
1 tablespoon cinnamon
½ cup chopped pecans

Dissolve yeast in water. Add eggs and melted butter and set aside. Combine ½ cup sugar, flour, and salt. Add to liquid mixture. Mix well but do not knead. Cover and refrigerate at least 1 hour.

Remove from refrigerator after dough has risen, and divide into 3 parts. Roll each part into a rectangular shape ¼-inch thick on a floured surface. Melt ½ stick butter and spread evenly over rectangles. Combine remaining ½ cup sugar and cinnamon; sprinkle evenly over 3 rectangles. Sprinkle each with chopped pecans. Roll each piece of dough like a jellyroll and cut into ¾-inch slices. Place in a greased container with sides touching and allow to rise in a warm place for 1½ hours. Bake at 400 degrees for 12–15 minutes. Cool slightly and frost with Cream Cheese Icing. Yield: 36 rolls

CREAM CHEESE ICING

1 stick butter, softened
1 (8-ounce) package cream cheese, softened
4 cups confectioners' sugar
1 teaspoon vanilla
2 tablespoons milk

Combine butter, cream cheese, confectioners' sugar, and vanilla. Add enough milk to achieve spreadable consistency.

WHEN DOUBLING A RECIPE,
NEVER DOUBLE THE AMOUNT OF SALT.

STICKY BUNS

2½ tablespoons unsalted butter
½ cup light brown sugar, divided
2 tablespoons light corn syrup
2 teaspoons honey
½ cup coarsely chopped pecans
1 (8-ounce) can crescent rolls
½ teaspoon cinnamon

Preheat oven to 375 degrees. Grease 9-inch cake pan. Melt butter in saucepan over low heat. Stir in ¼ cup sugar, corn syrup, and honey. Increase heat to medium, and stir until sugar melts and syrup boils. Pour syrup into prepared pan. Sprinkle with pecans. Unroll dough on floured surface; press perforations together. Roll dough to 8x12-inch rectangle. Sprinkle with remaining ¼ cup sugar and cinnamon. Roll long sides of rectangle, jellyroll style. Cut roll into 12 one-inch rounds. Place in syrup in pan. Bake 18–20 minutes. Cool in pan one minute; place plate over pan and invert onto plate. Spoon any syrup remaining over buns. Yield: 12 buns

Great idea

Give each guest a welcome basket with information about the wedding activities. Include city maps, local attactions, and snacks.

SHARI'S STRAWBERRY SHORTCAKE

9 eggs, separated
1 cup sugar, divided
½ cup vegetable oil
¼ cup vanilla yogurt
¼ cup frozen passion fruit concentrate, thawed
¾ cup cake flour

Preheat oven to 350 degrees. In medium bowl, whisk egg yolks and ½ cup sugar. Add oil, yogurt, and passion fruit concentrate; mix until blended. Gradually add flour and set aside. Beat egg whites with mixer on medium speed; gradually add remaining ½ cup sugar and beat until stiff peaks form. Add 2 tablespoons of egg whites into the yolk mixture; then fold in ½ of egg whites into yolk mixture with wooden spoon. Fold yolk mixture gently into remaining egg whites. Spoon batter into ungreased tube pan. Bake for 40–50 minutes. Place on wire rack to cool in pan. To release cake, run a knife around edge of pan. Frost cake.

A purchased angel food cake may be used. Yield: 16–20 servings

FROSTING

2 pints whipping cream, divided
6 tablespoons frozen passion fruit concentrate, thawed, divided
8 tablespoons sugar, divided
4 pints strawberries, washed and sliced
For garnish: whole strawberries with leaves

In a chilled bowl, whip 1 pint cream and 3 tablespoons concentrate with 4 tablespoons sugar. Repeat with remaining cream, concentrate, and sugar. Slice cake in half and place larger round on cake plate. Layer sliced strawberries on cake and in center hole and then ice with ½ the first batch of whipped cream mixture. Add another layer of strawberries and ice entire first cake layer with remaining ½ of first batch of whipped cream mixture. Stack other half of cake on top and fill hole with strawberries; ice sides and top of cake with second batch of whipped cream mixture; garnish with whole strawberries.

APPLE JUICE COOLER

¼ cup brown sugar
3 cups water
1 gallon apple juice
2 (6-ounce) cans frozen orange juice
2 liters ginger ale
For garnish: orange slices and mint

Dissolve sugar in water, apple juice, and orange juice over low heat. Cool and refrigerate. Add ginger ale and serve over crushed ice. Garnish with orange slices and mint. Yield: 1 gallon

FREEZE ICE CUBES WITH JUICE TO AVOID DILUTING FRUIT DRINKS. GARNISH ICE WITH FLOWERS AND FRUIT.

Home Wedding

Everyone loves a home wedding shared by a special gathering of family and friends. A garden ceremony is especially lovely followed by a sumptuous meal carefully prepared from favorite family recipes. Guests are welcomed by a wreath of fresh English boxwood hanging from cascading, cream satin ribbons. After the exchange of vows, a buffet lunch is served from the dining room table with antique silver serving pieces surrounding a massive stacked arrangement in a large silver punch bowl, edged in lime hydrangeas, white lilies, white roses, and hypericum berries, with soft blue delphinium feathering from the center. The wedding cake is served beside a sunny window in a wide entrance foyer on a round table skirted in taupe raw silk puddling on the floor topped with an embroidered white-work round linen cloth. The two-tiered Italian Cream Wedding Cake is decorated with tiny dots and the couple's new monogram and shares the table with white hydrangeas in a trumpet vase and an offering of chocolates.

Menu

Celebration Shrimp
Confetti Orzo
Spinach Madeline with Artichoke Topping
Mini Tomato Tarts
Raspberry Cheddar Cheesecake
Basil Biscuits
Italian Cream Wedding Cake

CELEBRATION SHRIMP

2 shallots, finely chopped
3 ribs celery, finely chopped
6 green onions, finely chopped
7 tablespoons butter, divided
½ pound fresh mushrooms, sliced
1 pound small fresh shrimp, peeled and deveined
Zest from 2 lemons
1 teaspoon salt
½ teaspoon white pepper
2 (3-ounce) packages cream cheese, softened
¼ cup finely chopped walnuts
3 tablespoons mayonnaise
1 teaspoon dry sherry
¼ cup half-and-half
3 tablespoons butter
1 cup coarse bread crumbs

Preheat oven to 350 degrees. With food processor, chop shallots, celery, and onions with quick on/off pulses and set aside. Heat skillet; add 4 tablespoons butter, shallots, celery, and onions. Cook on low heat until soft. Add mushrooms, shrimp, lemon zest, salt, and pepper. Stir well, remove from heat, and pour into 9x13-inch dish sprayed with nonstick cooking spray. With food processor, combine cream cheese, walnuts, mayonnaise, and sherry until smooth. Add half-and-half and process just to blend. Pour over shrimp mixture. Melt remaining 3 tablespoons butter; add crumbs and toss to coat. Sprinkle over top. Bake 15–20 minutes. Yield: 8 servings

CONFETTI ORZO

1 (16-ounce) package orzo
¼ cup each: diced green, red, yellow, and orange bell peppers
2 tablespoons olive oil

Cook orzo according to package directions. Sauté peppers for about 1½ minutes in olive oil. Combine orzo and bell peppers. Yield: 8 servings

SPINACH MADELINE WITH ARTICHOKE TOPPING

2 (16-ounce) packages frozen chopped spinach
1 onion, chopped
4 tablespoons butter
2 tablespoons flour
½ cup evaporated milk
¾ cup drained spinach liquid
1 teaspoon garlic salt
½ teaspoon black pepper
¼ teaspoon red pepper
1 teaspoon Worchestershire sauce
1 teaspoon Louisiana Hot Sauce
6 ounces shredded Monteray Jack cheese with jalapeños

Cook spinach according to package directions; drain and reserve liquid. Sauté onion in butter until soft. Add flour. Cook 5 minutes, stirring. Add milk and ¾ cup drained spinach liquid; cook until thickened. Add garlic salt, peppers, Worcestershire, and Hot Sauce. Add spinach and cheese. Add Artichoke Topping.

ARTICHOKE TOPPING

1 (6-ounce) can artichoke bottoms, finely minced
2 tablespoons butter, softened
1½ cups fresh bread crumbs
½ teaspoon lemon juice
⅛ teaspoon garlic salt

Mix all ingredients together to make a paste. Pat evenly onto Spinach Madeline. Bake at 350 degrees for 20–30 minutes. Yield: 8 servings

MINI TOMATO TARTS

1 (10-ounce) can Ro-Tel tomatoes, drained
1 cup mayonnaise
1 (3-ounce) package real bacon bits
1 cup shredded Swiss cheese
3 (1.9-ounce) packages mini filo shells, thawed

Preheat oven to 350 degrees. Combine tomatoes, mayonnaise, bacon bits, and cheese. Fill shells and bake for 10–15 minutes. Yield: 45 tarts

RASPBERRY CHEDDAR CHEESECAKE

½ sleeve round butter crackers, crushed
½ stick butter, softened
1 pound sharp Cheddar cheese, shredded
1 cup mayonnaise
2 tablespoons finely grated onion
1½ cups toasted and chopped pecans
1 teaspoon each: salt and red pepper
For garnish: raspberry jam, fresh raspberries, and mint

Combine butter and crackers. Press into greased springform pan with parchment-lined bottom. Combine cheese, mayonnaise, onion, pecans, salt, and pepper. Press on top of crust. Chill. Remove from pan. Top with raspberry jam, berries, and mint. Serve with round butter crackers. Yield: 30 servings

BASIL BISCUITS

1 stick butter, softened
4 cups biscuit mix
1 cup sour cream
¾ cup club soda
½ stick butter, melted
Dried basil

Preheat oven to 400 degrees. Cut butter into mix with a pastry blender. Stir in sour cream and club soda. Turn onto floured surface; shape into ball and knead 3 or 4 times. Roll out ½ inch thick. Cut out with 2-inch biscuit cutter and place on a lightly greased baking sheet. Bake 13–15 minutes. Brush with melted butter and sprinkle with dried basil. Yield: 36 biscuits

ITALIAN CREAM WEDDING CAKE

1 stick margarine, softened
½ cup shortening
2 cups sugar
5 eggs, separated
1 teaspoon baking soda
1 cup buttermilk
2 cups all-purpose flour
1 teaspoon salt
1 cup flaked coconut
1 cup chopped pecans
1 teaspoon vanilla

Preheat oven to 325 degrees. Grease and flour three 9-inch round cake pans and set aside. With mixer, cream margarine, shortening, and sugar. Beat well, and add egg yolks, one at a time, beating for one minute after each addition. Mix soda and buttermilk; add alternately with flour and salt to creamed mixture. Stir in coconut, pecans, and vanilla and set aside. Beat egg whites with mixer until stiff; fold into batter. Pour into pans, ⅔ full. Bake for 30 minutes. Remove to wire racks to cool and frost. For 2-tiered cake, repeat using 8-inch pans. You will have some batter left over.

CREAM CHEESE FROSTING

1 (8-ounce) package cream cheese, softened
1 stick margarine, softened
1 (1-pound) box confectioners' sugar
1 teaspoon vanilla
1 cup chopped pecans
½ cup flaked coconut

With mixer, beat cream cheese and margarine until light and fluffy. Add confectioners' sugar and vanilla. Beat until smooth. Stir in pecans and coconut. Spread between layers and frost sides and top of cake. Repeat recipe for frosting 8-inch cake. Yield: 12–16 servings

SEND THE COUPLE AWAY WITH A BASKET FILLED WITH BISCUITS, TOMATO TARTS, FRUITS, CHEESES, CRACKERS, AND WEDDING CAKE. ADD PERSONAL NOTES OF LOVE AND CONGRATULATIONS.

Buffet Reception

Time to kiss the bride, congratulate the groom, and wish God's blessings on their new life together. And it is also time to celebrate the marriage with fellowship and food. At this home reception, every area of the home is utilized—with cheese and fruits on majolica on the patio; tea, spritzer, and water in dramatic glass samovars on the buffet; entrées spread across the dining table; favorite desserts and a coffee bar in the family room; and, of course, a bakery wedding cake in the living room. Decorations are colorful flowers, ornamental cabbages, fruits, and vegetables with the fruit display; elegant loose arrangements on tall antique candlesticks in the dining room; and peach roses and trailing asparagus ferns in a tall, silver trumpet vase on a mirrored table in the family room—all pulled together with the central theme of the couple's new initial. With planning and organization, this reception is a delightful experience and memory for all.

Menu

Pork Tenderloin with rolls, Apricot Sauce, and Basil Mayonnaise

Grilled chicken tenders with Comeback Sauce

Shrimp Pasta

Spinach-Artichoke Squares

Tomato Bites

Pastry-Wrapped Brie

Cheese, Fruit, and Crackers

Berry Tea, Raspberry Spritzer

Coffee Bar

Pecan Pie Tarts

Bananas Foster

Death by Chocolate

Bakery Wedding Cake

Pork Tenderloin

2 pork tenderloins
1 (12-ounce) jar apricot jam
⅓ cup Dijon mustard
Salt and pepper to taste
2 tablespoons olive oil

Preheat oven to 450 degrees. Combine apricot jam and mustard in saucepan on low heat until melted. Salt, pepper, and oil tenderloins; brush with the jam and mustard glaze. Roast tenderloins for 45–60 minutes, glazing with the sauce and pan juices every 20 minutes until temperature reaches 180 degrees. Remove from oven and let rest. Serve with rolls, Apricot Sauce, and Basil Mayonnaise. Yield: 24 servings

APRICOT SAUCE

1 (12-ounce) jar apricot jam
⅓ cup Dijon mustard

Mix ingredients and heat on low until blended. Cool. Yield: 1¾ cups

BASIL MAYONNAISE

2 teaspoons chopped fresh basil
1½ cups mayonnaise

Stir basil into mayonnaise and chill. Yield: 1½ cups

Grilled Chicken Tenders with Comeback Sauce

20 chicken breast tenders
2 tablespoons lemon pepper seasoning
1 stick margarine

Preheat oven to 350 degrees. Wash chicken and sprinkle with lemon pepper. Place on a foil-lined baking sheet and dot with margarine. Cover with foil and bake for 20 minutes. Turn and bake 20 minutes more. Uncover and bake for another 10 minutes. Skewer each tender with a wooden skewer and serve warm or at room temperature. Yield: 20 servings

COMEBACK SAUCE

1 cup mayonnaise
½ teaspoon sugar
½ cup olive oil
½ cup ketchup
½ teaspoon onion powder
½ teaspoon black pepper
½ teaspoon salt
1 tablespoon Worcestershire sauce
5 drops Tabasco Sauce
2 teaspoons minced garlic
1 tablespoon horseradish mustard
2 tablespoons cold water

Combine all ingredients until well mixed. Yield: 2 cups

SERVE ROOM-TEMPERATURE FOODS ON LARGE SERVING TRAYS TO AVOID REPLENISHING WHEN GUESTS ARRIVE. SERVE DISHES IN DIFFERENT LOCATIONS TO AVOID CONGESTION AND TO ALLOW GUESTS TO MINGLE AND VISIT.

Shrimp Pasta

1½ sticks margarine

1 cup chopped onion

2 tablespoon dried parsley

1½ cups sliced fresh mushrooms

1 teaspoon salt

1 teaspoon black pepper

½ teaspoon white pepper

¼ teaspoon garlic powder

½ teaspoon Tony Chachere's Creole seasoning

1½ pounds fresh medium shrimp, peeled and deveined

1 (12-ounce) package fettuccini, cooked al dente and drained

1 tablespoon olive oil

1 (16-ounce) package processed cheese, cut into ½-inch pieces

1 (4-ounce) can chopped green chiles, drained

½ cup half-and-half

Preheat oven to 350 degrees. In a large skillet, melt margarine over medium-high heat. Add onion and cook for 5 minutes. Stir in parsley, mushrooms, salt, peppers, garlic powder, and Tony's seasoning. Pour mixture into a 9x13-inch baking dish and stir in shrimp, tossing gently to coat. Bake for 20 minutes, stirring occasionally. Cook fettuccini al dente. Add olive oil, cheese, green chiles, and half-and-half. Stir until melted and combined. Remove shrimp from oven; stir in fettuccini and cheese mixture until combined. Cover with foil and warm for 5 minutes. Yield: 20 small servings

Spinach-Artichoke Squares

2 (8-ounce) cans crescent rolls

1 (14-ounce) can artichoke hearts, drained and chopped

1 (9-ounce) box frozen spinach, thawed, squeezed, and drained

1 cup grated Parmesan cheese

¾ cup mayonnaise

¾ cup sour cream

For garnish: lemon zest

Heat oven to 375 degrees. Unroll dough into 4 long rectangles. Place crosswise in bottom and one inch up the sides of ungreased 10x15-inch pan to form crust. Seal perforations. Bake 10–12 minutes. Mix remaining ingredients and spread over crust. Bake 8–10 minutes or until topping is thoroughly heated. Cut into 2-inch squares. Garnish with lemon zest. Serve warm. Yield: 40 appetizers

Tomato Bites

1¼ cup Hellmann's mayonnaise

½ cup finely chopped fresh parsley

1 (4.3-ounce) package crumbled bacon bits

1 (1-pound) box Wheat Thins

1 pint grape tomatoes, cut in half and drained on paper towels

Mix together mayonnaise, parsley, and bacon bits. Spread on wheat thins and top with a tomato half, cut side down. Yield: 60 bites

PASTRY-WRAPPED BRIE

1 (8-ounce) can crescent rolls
1 (8-ounce) round Brie cheese
½ cup raspberry jam
½ teaspoon dried rosemary
½ cups chopped walnuts

Heat oven to 350 degrees. Unroll dough and press into 2 (7-inch) squares; seal perforations. Cut cheese horizontally to make 2 rounds. Do not remove rind. Place a cheese round, rind side down, in center of dough square. Spread with jam and sprinkle with rosemary and walnuts. Top with remaining cheese round, rind side up. With cookie cutter or knife, cut leaf shapes from corners of remaining dough square; set aside. Place remaining dough on top of cheese. Press dough around cheese folding top over bottom edges; press to seal. Place on ungreased cookie sheet. Place leaves on cookie sheet next to wrapped Brie. Bake leaves 8–11 minutes; remove from oven and cool. Bake wrapped cheese 25–30 minutes or until golden brown. Remove from cookie sheet; place on serving plate. Place leaves on top of wrapped cheese. Let stand 15 minutes before serving. Serve warm with fruit and water crackers. Yield: 24 servings

BERRY TEA

1 cup Nestea concentrate with lemon
3 cups mixed berry juice
2 cups orange juice
1½ teaspoons Crystal Light Lemonade mix
5 cups water

Mix all ingredients together and serve over ice. Yield: 2½ quarts

RASPBERRY SPRITZER

1 (2-quart) bottle raspberry juice
1 (2-liter) bottle ginger ale
To garnish: lemon and lime slices, raspberries, cranberries, and mint

Mix juice and ginger ale and serve over crushed ice. Garnish with citrus slices, berries, and mint. Yield: 16–20 servings

PECAN PIE TARTS

4 eggs, separated
2 cups sugar
6 tablespoons butter, melted
¼ teaspoon salt
1 cup raisins
1 cup chopped pecans
2 tablespoons vinegar
2 (1.9-ounce) packages mini filo shells

Preheat oven to 350 degrees. Combine egg yolks, sugar, butter, and salt. Add raisins, pecans, and vinegar; set aside. Beat egg whites with mixer to stiff peaks. Fold whites into yolk mixture. Put 1 teaspoon filling into each mini shell and bake 30 minutes. Yield: 30 tarts

FOR A WELCOMING SURPRISE, SPRINKLE ROSE PETALS IN THE SHAPE OF THE COUPLE'S INITIAL ON THE FRONT LAWN.

BANANAS FOSTER

½ stick butter, melted
1½ cups crushed vanilla wafers
½ cup caramel topping
1 teaspoon rum extract
¼ teaspoon ground cinnamon
2 medium bananas, cut into ⅛-inch slices
4 cups milk
3 (3.4-ounce) boxes instant banana pudding and pie
  filling mix
1½ (8-ounce) containers whipped topping, divided
For garnish: pesticide-free pansies

Melt butter and stir in crushed vanilla wafers; set aside. Combine caramel topping, rum extract, and cinnamon. Toss banana slices with caramel sauce until coated; set aside. Beat milk and pudding mixes with mixer until thickened. Fold in whipped topping. In individual juice glasses, layer 1 tablespoon vanilla wafer crumbs, 2 or 3 banana slices and a little sauce, and 3 tablespoons pudding. Repeat layers and end with a little sauce. Add a dollop of whipped topping and a pansy. Yield: 16 (6-ounce) servings

DEATH BY CHOCOLATE

1 (19.8-ounce) package brownie mix
1 teaspoon sugar, dissolved in 4 tablespoons prepared
  black coffee
4 cups milk
3 (3.4-ounce) boxes instant chocolate pudding mix
8 (1.4-ounce) Heath candy bars, crushed
½ cup slivered almonds, toasted and chopped
1 (8-ounce) container whipped topping

Bake brownies according to package directions. Cool. Punch holes in brownies with fork and pour in sugar-coffee mixture. Crumble brownies; set aside. Beat milk and pudding mixes with mixer until thickened; set aside. Combine candy and almonds. In individual juice glasses, layer 1 tablespoon brownie crumbles, 3 tablespoons pudding, 1 tablespoon candy and almond pieces, and 1 tablespoon whipped topping. Repeat and end with whipped topping, and sprinkle with candy and almonds. Yield: 16 (6-ounce) servings

Great ideas

PERSONALIZE THE PARTY

Greet guests at the front door with the couple's initial hanging from a satin ribbon on a green wreath.

Continue the "initial" theme by placing adhesive letters on miniature dessert glasses. Serve the dessert with a collection of antique demitasse spoons and garnish with chocolate hearts, fruits, or pesticide-free pansies.

Let Them Eat Cake

For a perfectly elegant, simple, and inexpensive afternoon reception, indulge guests with an array of the new couple's favorite cakes surrounding the exquisite wedding cake featuring layers of varying heights in fondant icing decorated with fresh flowers and ribbons. Guests may enjoy Red Velvet Cake, Lemon Icebox Cake, Caramel Cake, German Chocolate Cake, or Sweet Potato Cake with Mint Tea, Coffee Punch, or coffee. The serving table is decorated with streaming tendrils of trailing tree ferns, and cakes are decorated with fresh flowers in water vials, fruits, lemon curls, white and dark chocolate-dipped strawberries, and chocolate initials and names. To make selections easier, cakes are labeled with tags attached to small, golden heart Christmas ornaments. After visiting with family and friends and enjoying desserts, the couple may depart with a basket of sandwiches, savories, and cake and be on their way to a sweet honeymoon and life together.

Top it off

CHOCOLATE-COVERED STRAWBERRIES

Melt candy coating in the microwave on defrost at two-minute intervals. Dip strawberries with leaves intact (that have been washed and thoroughly dried) into the chocolate, and allow them to harden on wax paper. Dipped strawberries may be refrigerated, but let them come to room temperature before serving or using as decorations on cakes.

CHOCOLATE LETTERS

Create chocolate initials or names by pouring melted chocolate into a squeeze bottle with a writing tip. Use the bottle as a pen to trace patterns placed beneath wax paper with chocolate. When letters and names are set, place them on the cake.

Use golden Christmas ornament hearts with labels attached by ribbon bows to identify the cakes.

Adorn cakes with ribbons and flowers, Praline Topping, and fresh raspberries with lemon curls and mint to create beauty, color, and texture.

RED VELVET CAKE

1½ sticks butter, softened
2¼ cups sugar
3 eggs
6 tablespoons red food coloring
3 tablespoons cocoa
1½ teaspoons vanilla
1½ teaspoons salt
1½ cups buttermilk
3⅓ cups all-purpose flour
1½ teaspoons vinegar
1½ teaspoons baking soda

Preheat oven to 350 degrees. Cream butter and sugar with mixer. Add eggs, one at a time, beating after each. Beat in food coloring, cocoa, vanilla, and salt. Add buttermilk and flour alternately. Combine vinegar and soda; add to batter and beat well. Pour into 3 greased and floured 9-inch pans and bake for 30–40 minutes. Cool in pans before turning out on wire racks. Frost with Cream Cheese Frosting. Yield: 12–16 servings

CREAM CHEESE FROSTING

1 stick margarine, softened
1 (8-ounce) package cream cheese, softened
1 (1-pound) box confectioners' sugar
1 teaspoon vanilla

Cream margarine and cream cheese with mixer. Beat in sugar and vanilla.

LEMON ICEBOX CAKE

1 (18.25-ounce) box lemon supreme cake mix
½ cup oil
1 cup water
3 eggs
For garnish: fresh raspberries, lemon rind curls, and mint

Preheat oven to 350 degrees. Combine cake mix, oil, water, and eggs; beat with mixer for 2 minutes. Pour into 3 greased and floured 8-inch cake pans. Bake for 18–20 minutes. Allow to cool. Spread remaining Filling between layers of cake. Spread Icing over sides and top of cake. Refrigerate one day before serving. Garnish with raspberries, lemon curls, and mint. Yield: 12–16 servings

FILLING

2 (14-ounce) cans sweetened condensed milk
¾ cup fresh lemon juice

Stir sweetened condensed milk and lemon juice together. Reserve ½ cup for Icing.

ICING

½ cup reserved Filling
1 (8-ounce) container whipped topping

Combine reserved Filling and whipped topping.

GERMAN CHOCOLATE CAKE

1 (8-ounce) package German sweet chocolate
½ cup boiling water
1 cup butter
2 cups sugar
4 egg yolks, unbeaten
1 teaspoon vanilla
½ teaspoon salt
1 teaspoon baking soda
2½ cups cake flour
1 cup buttermilk
4 egg whites, stiffly beaten

Preheat oven to 350 degrees. Melt chocolate in boiling water. Cool and set aside. Cream butter and sugar until fluffy with mixer. Add egg yolks, one at a time; beat well after each addition. Add melted chocolate and vanilla. Mix well. Sift together salt, soda, and flour. Add alternately with buttermilk to chocolate mixture, beating well. Beat until smooth. Fold into beaten egg whites. Pour into two 9-inch or three 8-inch greased and floured pans lined on bottoms with wax paper. Bake for 30–40 minutes. Cool. Frost between layers and on sides and top of cake with Coconut-Pecan Frosting. Yield: 12–16 servings

COCONUT-PECAN FROSTING

1 (12-ounce) can evaporated milk
1½ cups sugar
¾ cup margarine
4 egg yolks, lightly beaten
1½ teaspoons vanilla
1 (7-ounce) package sweetened coconut
1½ cups chopped pecans

Mix milk, sugar, margarine, egg yolks, and vanilla in a large saucepan. Cook over medium heat for 12 minutes or until thickened and golden brown, stirring constantly. Remove from heat. Add coconut and pecans; mix well. Cool to room temperature.

CARAMEL CAKE

1 (18.25-ounce) box yellow cake mix
1 cup water
½ cup oil
4 eggs
1 teaspoon vanilla

Preheat oven to 350 degrees. Beat cake mix, water, and oil with a mixer on medium speed for 2 minutes. Beat in eggs and vanilla. Pour into two 9-inch or three 8-inch greased and floured pans. Bake for 20–23 minutes. Spread Easy Caramel Frosting between layers and on sides and top of cake. Just before serving, pour Praline Topping over iced cake. Yield: 16–20 servings

EASY CARAMEL FROSTING

½ cup butter
1 cup light brown sugar, packed
1 cup evaporated milk
2 cups confectioners' sugar
1 teaspoon vanilla

Melt butter in a medium saucepan. Add brown sugar and bring to a boil, stirring for 1 minute. Remove from heat, and add evaporated milk. Return saucepan to low heat, and bring to a boil. Remove from heat, and cool slightly or until candy thermometer reads 110 degrees. Beat in sugar with wooden spoon or mixer until frosting is thick. If too thin, add a little more sugar. Remove from heat; add vanilla. Place saucepan in a bowl of ice water, and beat until frosting reaches spreading consistency.

PRALINE TOPPING

1 pint whipping cream
1 (1-pound) box light brown sugar
2 tablespoons margarine
2 cups pecan halves

Microwave whipping cream and brown sugar 13 minutes on high. Stir in margarine and pecans. Stir for about 6 minutes.

THE WEDDING CAKE IS USUALLY THE BRIDE'S FAVORITE CAKE WITH HER CHOICE OF ICING AND DECORATIONS. THE GROOM'S CAKE IS A CHOCOLATE OR CARAMEL CAKE, BUT MAY ALSO BE HIS CHOICE OF DESSERTS. THE BRIDE'S FAMILY PROVIDES BOTH CAKES.

SWEET POTATO CAKE WITH LEMON CREAM CHEESE FROSTING

2½ cups self-rising flour
2 teaspoons cinnamon
½ teaspoon nutmeg
¾ cup raisins
1 cup toasted and chopped walnuts
2 cups sugar
4 eggs
1 cup plus 2 tablespoons vegetable oil, divided
2 cups baked and mashed sweet potatoes
⅓ cup sweetened shredded coconut

Preheat oven to 325 degrees. Combine flour, cinnamon, and nutmeg with a wire whisk and set aside. Mix raisins and nuts with 2 tablespoons oil and ¼ cup of flour mixture; toss well and set aside. Combine sugar and remaining 1 cup oil with a wooden spoon. Add eggs one at a time, beating well after each addition. Add remaining flour mixture and stir just until combined. Thoroughly mix in mashed sweet potatoes and coconut. Gently mix in floured raisins and nuts. Pour batter into two 9-inch greased and floured pans and bake for 25 minutes. Cake will begin to pull away from sides of pan. Cool in pan on a wire rack for 10 minutes. Turn cakes out and place them topside up on the wire rack to cool.

LEMON CREAM CHEESE FROSTING

4 cups confectioners' sugar
2 (8-ounce) packages cream cheese, softened
Pinch of salt
3 tablespoons lemon juice
1 tablespoon lemon zest
3 tablespoons evaporated milk
6 tablespoons toasted and chopped walnuts
For garnish: 3 tablespoons toasted and chopped walnuts

Combine the sugar, cream cheese, salt, lemon juice, and zest with a mixer. Mix until smooth and creamy. Add milk to make the frosting easier to spread. Place first layer topside down with a dollop of icing to hold the layer in place on a cake plate. Spread about half of frosting on top and sides of first layer. Place second layer on top of iced first layer. Frost the sides and top. Sprinkle top and sides of cake with toasted walnuts. Yield: 16 servings

MINT TEA

7 Bigelow Plantation Mint tea bags
2 tubs Crystal Light Lemonade

Bring 8 cups water to a boil, add tea bags, cover, and turn off heat; steep for 15 minutes. Add lemonade and stir to dissolve. Add 8 cups cold water. Yield: 1 gallon

COFFEE PUNCH

½ cup very strong hazelnut coffee, brewed
2 cups sugar, dissolved in hot coffee
3 cups milk
2 cups half-and-half
1 teaspoon vanilla
½ cup kahlúa

Mix all ingredients, and freeze flat in gallon zipper bags. Take out of freezer one hour before serving, and crush with a spoon to make slushy. Yield: 12–16 servings

Puppy Love

Although this table is designed with children in mind, it will bring out the kid in everyone. The design is bright and colorful, and the foods are simple pick-up items that taste great and will keep children content as their parents enjoy the reception. The color scheme is lime and pink, and the food offerings and decorations follow suit. Everything is served from rustic urns and glass rounds stacked and placed randomly on the table. Sugar Cookies, shaped and decorated as pink cats and lime dogs, beg to be chosen, and pink cupcakes with sprinkles and Puppy Dog Cakes with hot pink bows are displayed amidst a myriad of candy, lollipops, Marshmallow Pops, and popcorn in cones. Mini Cheeseburgers, Mini Hot Dogs, and Chicken Nuggets are perfect for small hands. Children are sure to have fun and remember this fantasy table designed especially for them.

Menu

MINI CHEESEBURGERS
MINI HOT DOGS
CHICKEN NUGGETS
POPCORN
STRAWBERRIES AND GREEN GRAPES
MARSHMALLOW POPS
PUPPY DOG CAKES AND CUPCAKES
CATS AND DOGS SUGAR COOKIES
JELLY BEANS, RIBBON CANDY, AND
    LOLLIPOPS
CHERRY LIMEADE

MINI CHEESEBURGERS

1 pound ground beef
1 teaspoon oregano
2 teaspoons Worcestershire sauce
3 slices American cheese
1 dozen small dinner rolls
Lettuce

Preheat oven to 350 degrees. Combine beef, oregano, and Worcestershire. Form into twelve 2-inch patties. Place on a foil-lined baking sheet and bake 15–20 minutes. Place meat, ¼ slice of cheese, and lettuce on each bun. Yield: 12 burgers

MINI HOT DOGS

2 (8-ounce) packages crescent rolls
1 (14-ounce) package beef smokies

Preheat oven to 375 degrees. Separate each package of dough into 8 triangles. Cut each triangle into 3 parts. Wrap each smokie in a triangle. Bake for 12–15 minutes on an ungreased cookie sheet. Yield: 48 hot dogs

CHICKEN NUGGETS

12 boneless, skinless chicken strips
Salt and pepper to taste
3 cups Rice Krispies, crushed

Preheat oven to 350 degrees. Wash chicken and pat dry. Cut into nugget-size pieces; salt and pepper each piece and roll in Rice Krispies. Place on a greased, foil-lined baking sheet, and bake 20 minutes. Yield: 36 nuggets

MARSHMALLOW POPS

½ (1-pound) package chocolate melts
½ (1-pound) package marshmallows
Sprinkles and sucker sticks

Melt chocolate in microwave at 2-minute intervals on defrost until melted. Place a sucker stick into each marshmallow and dip into chocolate; drizzle with sprinkles. Yield: 24 pops

PUPPY DOG CAKES AND CUPCAKES

1 (18.25-ounce) package yellow cake mix, prepared according to direcions

For dog, place 2 cupcakes, without liners, side by side on plate. Using a large star tip, pipe frosting over one side of both cupcakes and then over the other sides to resemble the body and face. Pipe on nose, ears, and tail. Add a pink bow and tongue and black eyes and a nose with the small writing tip. For cupcakes, pipe on frosting with the large star tip. Yield: 6 dogs or 12 cupcakes

VANILLA BUTTERCREAM FROSTING

1 stick unsalted butter, softened
1 (2-pound) bag confectioners' sugar, divided
¼ cup milk
1 teaspoon vanilla
¼ teaspoon almond flavoring

Cream butter and 1 pound sugar with mixer. Add milk and flavorings. Gradually add remaining sugar. Beat in food coloring, if desired. Yield: enough for 3 dogs or 12 cupcakes

CHOCOLATE BUTTERCREAM FROSTING

3 sticks unsalted butter, softened
2 tablespoons milk
9 ounces semi-sweet chocolate, melted
1 teaspoon vanilla
¼ teaspoon almond flavoring
2¾ cups confectioners' sugar

Beat butter with mixer until creamy. Beat in milk, slightly cooled melted chocolate, and flavorings. Beat in sugar. Yield: enough for 3 dogs or 12 cupcakes

ADD FLAIR TO THE "JUST FOR KID'S" TABLE WITH RIBBONS OF COORDINATING COLORS IN VARIOUS WIDTHS AND PATTERNS. TIE RIBBONS AROUND THE CUPCAKE LINERS, LOLLIPOP STICKS, AND TO THE CHERRY LIMEADE JAR TOP— JUST FOR FUN!

SUGAR COOKIES

2 cups all-purpose flour
1½ teaspoons baking powder
¼ teaspoon salt
½ cup butter, softened
1 cup sugar
1 egg
1 tablespoon evaporated milk
1½ teaspoons vanilla

Preheat oven to 375 degrees. Sift flour, baking powder, and salt, and set aside. Cream butter and sugar. Add egg, milk, and vanilla. Add flour mixture to creamed mixture. Roll dough into 2 balls, wrap in wax paper; chill. Roll out dough on a floured surface ¼ inch thick, and cut into desired shapes. Bake 10–15 minutes; do not brown. Cool on a wire rack and brush with Icing. Yield: 16–24 cookies

ICING

¼ stick margarine, melted
2 cups confectioners' sugar
¼ cup evaporated milk
½ teaspoon vanilla

Mix all ingredients together and brush over cookies.

CHERRY LIMEADE

2 (12-ounce) cans frozen limeade
1 (10-ounce) jar maraschino cherries, not drained
1 (2-liter) bottle lemon-lime carbonated beverage

Prepare limeade according to directions. Stir in cherries and juice. Pour in lemon-lime drink just before serving over crushed ice. Yield: 1 gallon, 30 servings

Index of Parties

The menus, recipes, and great ideas in *Easy Parties and Wedding Celebrations* are interchangeable. Inspiration for your next event may come from several parties combined with a favorite recipe of your own or an entire party with all the decorations and great ideas included. The menus are adaptable for any brunch, lunch, or dinner, whether it's a party, a celebration, a few ladies for lunch, or a monthly supper club for dinner. This is a listing of the types of parties for a quick reference. Be innovative and enjoy!

Credits

Homes

Gail and Jan Collins—Easter Luncheon, Hen Party, and Flamingo Brunch

Judith and Eugene Douglass—Anniversary Dinner

Mary Graves—Mother's Day Garden Luncheon

Gale and Jeff Hammond—Victorian Valentine Brunch

Madalyn and Steve Hindman—Formal Holiday Dinner and Home Wedding

Maggi and Lee Lampton—Poolside Graduation Brunch and Meet the Family

Sarah and Phil Nelson—Autumn Dinner

Gayla and Bill Stone—Hydrangea Brunch

Tricia and Alan Walters—Honoring Father

Jean and Palmer Wilks—Christmas Buffet

Couples Honored

Melissa and Stewart Boyd

Page and Grant Callen

Allen and Doug Cunningham

Lauren and Luke Eaton

Kate and Justin Estess

Emily and David Harbarger

Rachael and Claude Harbarger

Harper and David Jones

Ann and Daniel McNair

Emily and Frank Porter

Sarabeth and Bryan Segars

Cakes

Robyn Farber—Mini Wedding Cakes

Faye Hoyt—Italian Cream Wedding Cake

Carrie Peters Montgomery—Wedding Cake

Lou Van Velkinburgh—Lou's Petit Fours

Photographers

Ron Blaylock

Author photographs

Honoring Father, pages 34–39

Autumn Dinner, pages 52–55

Marry Me Dinner, pages 90–91

Nuts and Bolts Shower, pages 124–127

Buffet Reception, pages 168–173

Let Them Eat Cake, pages 174–179

Puppy Love, pages 180–185

Pages 4 bottom left, 8, 22, 86, 88 top left and bottom right, 102, 103, 155, 156, and 157

Photographers (continued)

Greg Campbell

Back jacket left and right

Happy Birthday Hats, pages 10–15

Purses and Pearls Luncheon, pages 16–19

Poolside Graduation Brunch, pages 30–33

Sip and See the New Baby, pages 46–51

Southern Fall Buffet, pages 56–58

Paris Chic Debutante Party, pages 66–68 and 71

Christmas Buffet, pages 72–77

Victorian Valentine Brunch, pages 84–85

Meet the Family, pages 94–97

Engagement Announcement, pages 104–109

Couples' Dinner Shower, pages 110–113

Doves and Birdcages, pages 114–119

Hen Party, pages 120–121 and 123

Flamingo Brunch, pages 128–133

Swan Luncheon, pages 134–139

Favorite Ladies' Luncheon, pages 140–145

Tying the Knot, pages 146–151

Rehearsal Dinner, pages 152–154

Hydrangea Brunch, pages 158–159, 162, and 163

Home Wedding, page 164–165

Pages 2, 8 top right, 20, 23, 28, 29, 62, 88 top right and bottom left, 92, 93, 100 top, and 188

Shane Carr

Anniversary Dinner, pages 60–61 and 63–65

Bonnie Dickerson

Pages 21, 36, 69, 70, 87, 116 center, and 122

Tempy Segrest

Front cover

Back jacket center

Mother's Day Garden Luncheon, pages 24–27

Fourth of July Celebration, pages 40–45

Will You Be My Bridesmaid?, pages 98–101

Pages 8 top left, 12 top right, 59, 62 bottom, page 68 top left, 116 top left and bottom right, and 160

David Wiggins

Formal Holiday Dinner, pages 78–83

Page 8 bottom right

Recipe Credits

Kathryn Allman
Elaine Atkins
Eric Bach
Linda Kay Barbour
Rita Black
Sandy Black
Candy Blue
Marty Bowen
Emily Hines Burgess
Sylvia Burnham
Lynda Butler
Jeff Byrd
Lena Causey
Gail Collins
Melinda Courtney
Lynne Cunningham
Judy Davis
Kathryn Davis
Judith Douglass
Jean Easterling
Bette Fair
Robyn Farber
Joan B. Ferguson

Peggy Foggin
Billie Jean Giffin
Pam Glover
Gale Hammond
Karis Harbarger
Linn Harris
Tony Harris
Barri Haskins
Rosie Henderson
Madalyn Hindman
Carolyn Hodges
Linda Hogue
Katy Houston
Bill Hulsey
Joyce Jones
Charlotte Kidd
Maggi Lampton
Leila Lane
Beverly Lawrence
Mary Ellen Lawrence
Wesla Sullivan Leech
Davina Levy
Becky Lowther

Pat Lyon
Sandra Maris
Gwen Marsalis
Teresa McCarthy
Mary Jane McDaniel
Patty Mitchell
Shelia Moore
Shari Ong
Melissa Ridgway
Shirley Riley
Glenda Robinson
Johnnie Roland
Melanie Roper
Penny Roper
Amy Ross
Pat Ross
Sue Russ
Sarabeth Segars
Beth Shivers
Evelyn Slay
Lynn Slay
Jane Smith
Ruth Smith

Susan Spicer
Sue Ann Stewart
Margarita Stanford
Pat Stockett
Gayla Stone
Bobbye Strickland
Melanie Taylor
Arlette Thompson
Grace Toler
Lou Van Velkinburgh
Charla Walker
Tricia Walters
Melanie Ward
Marian Ware
Kim Waters
Mickey Watkins
Jean Wilks
Helen Williams
Robin Wise
Linda Wolfe
Ida Yerger
Beth Young
Debbie Zischke

Index